Jette Cuisine

By

Robert Martin

Published by Superwater Ltd

Robert Martin is a classic *Pisces*, with two fish swimming in opposite directions. He has an engineering degree from Cambridge and a teaching qualification from Oxford.

The engineering fish has swum ever deeper from construction of the Thames Barrier in the mid-70s through to subsea construction offshore Aberdeen and worldwide today.

The other fish is musical, playing the French Horn (surely the most technical of instruments) including the original run of *Jesus Christ Superstar* and touring with the *Albion Ensemble*.

Robert is fifty years to the day older than Brooklyn Beckham. He lives in rural Aberdeenshire with his wife, three daughters, and a garden full of fish.

ISBN 0-9541613-00

First Edition
Published by Superwater Ltd
2001

For My Family

who've eaten and enjoyed this

Aperitif
(Incisors)

I don't really like cooking.

So why on earth would I want to write a book about it?

And why for pity's sake would you want to read it?

I'll take the second question first if you don't mind:
- Because you want to able to cook a meal in 10 minutes, without your kitchen looking like a bomb's hit it.
- Because you know what you like, and want to eat what you like.
- Because you want to know how to make a meal out of all the odd quantities of ingredients left over from the dinner party you gave the night before.
- Because you don't like all the additives they put in food these days and want to be in control of what you eat.
- Because you're a student who doesn't want to starve or go bankrupt before graduating.
- Because you've a houseful of food but no idea what to eat this evening.
- Because you want to eat a high / low carbohydrate / protein / cholesterol diet.
- Because you don't see why - as a single parent in a minimal bed-sit - your child should grow up under-nourished.
- Because you've never cooked.
- Because you know vegetables are good for you, and you wish they'd taste good.
- Because you don't like washing up.
- Because you like cooking and want to learn some new tricks.
- Because you don't have money to burn.
- Because you're unique.

Any of the above answers will do. Any one will justify your reading this book.

Why me?

- Because I love food.
- Because I grew out of play-dough.
- Because food is universal.
- Because cooking must be simple to be universal.
- Because conventional cooking creates too many rules and obstacles.
- Because conventional cooking doesn't use modern ingredients to make life simpler.
- Because it's about time something so simple and universal was written down.
- Because it's too important to be left to the Purveyors of Party Food.

So it's You and Me then.

Table of Contents
(Happy Diners)

FOR STARTERS
Recipes Make Cooking Harder

In a world of recipe books, this is a cookbook.

It is intended for people who like their food and have other things to do with their time. Which I reckon includes most of us. Specialist chefs need not apply.

I'm always amazed when people say they can't cook. After all, they know what they like to eat, they can specify how they like their burger done and with what toppings, so they can obviously taste and understand different ingredients.

Of course, with some people it's just a ruse to get out of having to "do the cooking", and they're quite capable of it when they have to. Or, for whatever reason, they're not interested – which I find difficult to understand in anyone who professes to like eating. Since we all have to eat to survive, we might as well enjoy it, and who better to decide what we like than ourselves, from which it is only a small step to making it the way we like it.

If we ask people *why* they say they can't cook, we'll get all sorts of answers. Sometimes specific reasons, such as "I always burn everything" (which is just down to trying too hard: don't cook for so long), or "I can't even boil an egg". Boiling an egg is actually quite difficult, certainly more so than anything we're going to attempt in this book. Why so difficult? Two reasons:

    a) The ideal boiled egg has a firm white and a soft yolk, and you cannot get the white firm all through without starting to harden the yolk; because eggs are egg-shaped, and the yolk doesn't rest in the middle. Just a fact of life.

    b) Everyone knows what a boiled egg should be like.

So don't take any notice of some of our more notorious TV chefs who tell us this is the way to a perfect boiled egg: the "perfect" egg – one that cannot be faulted – does not exist. It never has, and it never will (at least not until we have developed intelligent microwaves, or genetically modified the egg), so the best that can be done is the one that best suits your personal taste. You're doing it, it's your taste that counts, no-one's else.

Eggs are particularly easy to fault: "Oooh, my white's all runny" or "Pass the butter, my yolk's gone hard". But the same applies to anything else we may cook: there's no such thing as perfection. If someone wants to find fault, they can, and that's their problem. As long as we focus on making tasty food that we would like to eat ourselves, and avoid anybody's dislikes or allergies, we won't go far wrong.

Now almost every cookbook since Mrs Beeton ("if the larder is empty, take two turkeys...") has been based on recipes. But are recipes really necessary? What did we do pre-Beeton?

Imagine that we're about to prepare a meal: what do we think of first? The most basic thoughts are likely to include:
- **What do we like?** No point in serving it if folk won't eat it.
- **What do we want?** We probably fancy a change from what we ate yesterday.
- **What have I got?** Or do I want to go shopping.
- **How long have I got?** Delete "banquet" if I've only got 10mins.

So we kick these questions around for a while and come up with a few ideas.

But instead of going on from there, we pick up the Recipe Book. And we find all sorts of information arranged in quite a different manner. It's listed under fancy titles like *Navarin of Lamb* or *Lemon Syllabub*, which give little guidance. We get a nice picture showing the end product, but since we don't eat photographs, we're none the wiser.

Let's assume that we've cleared this hurdle and arrived at something we want to prepare. Next comes the list of ingredients, and the fun really starts. We are drawn into a mysterious world of *fl oz's* and *tbsps*, *gms* and *mls*, so that straightaway we are distracted from the food we are to prepare. What is a *tbsp* anyway? Your tablespoon or mine? Heaped or level? How heaped (cocoa stacks higher than sugar)? And so on. But it is clearly important: the recipe has specified half a tbsp of this and 7oz of that, so if we get it wrong, will the dish be ruined? Who knows?

I have in front of me someone's soup recipe (picked at random) which includes:

- 15-16fl oz natural yoghurt
- 5 egg yolks
- Salt & black pepper
- 2 level tbsps chopped mint
- ½oz unsalted butter.

These are quantities for 6 people. So what are we to do with the 5 egg yolks if we're serving 4 (or 8)? Likewise the chopped mint; and is it dried, how finely is it chopped, both of which will make a big difference to how much goes in a level tbsp. How are we going to level the tbsp without scraping most of the mint onto the floor? Have we got a recipe that uses 5 egg whites? Why unsalted butter when we're adding salt & pepper anyway (unspecified quantities, are these unimportant)? It's more expensive than salted butter, so do we keep it in the fridge specially so that we can add ½oz to some soup? And why are they so relaxed about the quantity of yoghurt, are they trying to make us ill?

We can poke this sort of fun at almost any recipe, and you're probably thinking that all these questions can be answered with a bit of common sense. I agree. But if so, we're a long way towards not requiring the recipe at all.

And why do today's recipes call for unnatural quantities like 175gm of this or 225gm of that? Because they mean 6oz or 8oz. Except they're not exact conversions. So the recipe writer's got the quantities wrong anyway.

And as we read down our list of ingredients, there is always something we don't have in the store cupboard. Instead of cooking we're now detectives hunting down our ingredients in the supermarket long before we start to prepare the dish. Can we substitute any of the ingredients or leave them out, or will the dish be ruined? The recipe is unclear. And assuming we are successful in our search, we end up with a half-used ingredient that will clutter up the back of the cupboard for years, or which we will throw away when it rots.

Now we can get on with all the blending, gradual beating in, simmering, continuous stirring to avoid curdling, thickening, all that gadgetry – and this is only the soup. Has it ever struck you how the simplest tasks, written in recipe-speak, become complex and fraught with risk? Risk of what?

RISK OF IT GOING WRONG.

But how do we know it's wrong? Because we've got a photograph of it looking right, and ours doesn't look anything like that, so it must be wrong.

The photograph raises the art of false expectations to new heights. It needs to: the chances are it was the main reason we chose the recipe (and indeed bought the book) in the first place. There are skilled professionals who photograph food to best advantage, giving it make-up, shine, special lighting and so on. They do a fine job. So we shouldn't be disappointed when our result doesn't match the photograph, because the recipe doesn't contain instructions like "chill to eliminate steam and then spray with enamel paint".

I am sure that "disappointment" doesn't fully describe our emotions if we've chosen a spectacular dish for a dinner party largely on the basis if its appearance, and it doesn't come up to expectations. It probably tastes absolutely fine, something the photograph doesn't convey.

There are many other ways of raising false expectations, which in turn lead to false failures. The oldest one is "You don't make pastry like my mother's". Well of course you don't: haven't you noticed how people's handshakes are all different? So their pastry mixing won't be the same either. Not wrong, just different.

So what has the recipe given us:
• Lavish photography to raise our expectations, in order to dash them at the end.
• Ingredient lists that would tax a scientist.
• Shopping trips for the inevitable thing we haven't got.
• Instructions in professional jargon to make us feel small.

I suppose my main objection to recipes is that they create arbitrary rules where free expression should reign and no more than a bit of guidance is needed. They serve a purpose if we want to create "classic dishes", such as *Hollandaise Sauce* or a *Soufflé*. But why would we want to make a sauce which is bland, technically difficult, and invented by someone long since dead when the world has moved on? Would they have come up with that if they'd had today's ingredients available? And what is a soufflé other than gassy scrambled egg that's climbed out of its pot? The judging standard is how far it's risen, and since nowadays there are various "foolproof" versions, I regard soufflés as little more than a cheap prank.

Wait a minute: let's go back to where we were before we picked up the recipe book. We had some ideas about what we would cook, based on what we had and what people would like, before we got distracted. Well, **the aim of this book is to give us the confidence to go straight from that point to the meal on the table,** without making the kitchen look as though it's been hit by a bomb, and without anyone starving meantime.

We won't want to be consulting this book while we're cooking, having to wipe our hands clean or get the pages messy. So I've tried to write in such a way that it can be read as a book in its own right, keeping all the main ideas simple and clear, so that they are easy to apply in the kitchen. This will include ideas about combining ingredients, that you may think come pretty close to being recipes; I make no apologies for this because you deserve a bit more than plain "Do Your Own Thing", and anyway I'll be leaving quantities up to you. I'll be starting with the basic *Jette Cuisine* concept, and then fleshing it out with more detail afterwards. Miscellaneous chapters follow including ideas on taste combinations and fixing disasters.

I've packed quite a lot of information into each chapter; if you find there's too much to take in first time through, read the chapter again rather than going straight on. It's not written as a thriller. But don't get hung up on anything either.

Much of what I'm writing seems to me to be so simple and obvious (like the bit about boiled eggs) that I wonder whether it's worth writing down at all. Will you read it and say "Oh I know *that*", and am I wasting my time writing, your time reading? I've repeatedly asked myself this question, but concluded that I've spoken to enough people who don't find it obvious, and, after all, cooking *should* be simple and obvious.

Unlike the TV chefs, who seem to go to so much trouble to make things messy and complex. A cynic might suggest that they're trying to justify their own existence by making it all appear harder than it needs to be. Even when they're at their simplest, they can never resist adding that bottle of wine or pint of cream. Now any fool can make something tasty by buying the most expensive ingredients and giving no thought to how much cholesterol they pour down their throat. The rest of us live in the real world of budgets and blood pressure. Entertainment it may be, education it is not.

If I seem to be having a bit of a go at the folk in white coats, don't worry, I'll keep at it where appropriate throughout this book, although the worst is over. By now, you'll scarcely believe that I have a lot of respect for chefs, their skills and their profession. I love eating out, and I wouldn't swap with them. But they have a different agenda to those of us at home: they have professional staff to support them (and whom they have to keep in check), and they must always look for new ways of persuading us to part with our hard-earned cash. This may take the form of highly artistic presentation, or eclectic and fussy ingredients, neither of which I'd bother with at home. This sets them apart as something special and we love them for it.

But they're human too. We've all eaten things in restaurants that we know we could have cooked better ourselves, so we shouldn't get locked into thinking that their way is necessarily best. Indeed because of their background, I think chefs are especially unqualified to comment on home cooking in general, although no doubt they can cook at home. All right for dinner parties, but not for the 99% other meals we eat every day.

My qualifications? Only that I have been cooking without recipes, as student, man-about-town, husband, father, for 30yrs now, and not poisoned anyone. This is longer than some of our TV chefs have been on the planet. I have had no formal training, so I don't carry that baggage. I have a busy daytime job like most of us, so I can't spend long on what I cook. (I'm an engineer by profession, so at least I understand the mechanics.) I get more compliments than insults, which may just mean that I have very polite friends and family, or it may be something they ate. Our children have regularly eaten and enjoyed a range of healthy food (though they'll also eat junk like the best of us); better still they now knock up their own meals to their own taste. My thanks to them (and to The Better Half) for enjoying what I put in front of them.

I've had my disasters like everyone: my most memorable was trying to cook spaghetti during the 10min starter, which turned out to last half an hour. By this time the spaghetti looked like a floor mop soaked in wallpaper paste, and tasted much the same. Learn to ride your own disasters, you can generally sort them before serving (I'll give you some tips on this), there are very few which are terminal.

My final defence is that this book is not about making you cook "my way", but about you finding your own way. I'm sure there are things in here that won't suit you; hopefully there will be much that does.

Enough background and backbiting, let's cook!

JETTE CUISINE
Quicker Than Convenience Food.

Jette Cuisine was born underwater.

One Saturday morning some years ago, I'd taken the children for a swim and was passing the time with a few gentle lengths, when I heard a voice "Would you do a cookery class?" Not having my lenses in, it took a while to realise this question was directed at me. Then I recognised the swimmer as having come to a dinner party with us some time before; she was doing her lengths in the opposite direction.

"Just one evening, we could call it Perfect Pasta." I'd cooked three different dishes for the pasta course that evening, and my memory was still fairly fresh, so I accepted. All this took place in 5sec bursts over a number of lengths and between mouthfuls of chlorine, but nothing prepared me for the sudden intake of pool when she said "Oh good, we've got the chef of the new Italian Restaurant doing one on Italian food as well". The idea of my telling a Sicilian how to cook pasta caused me to think again about my immediate future.

A few lengths later, I'd made up my mind: definitely not pasta, but as I cook in an unconventional way without too many complaints, I might as well talk about it when asked. Everyone should have one cookery class in them, and this could be mine. And so *Jette Cuisine* was born.

It had been a long pregnancy. I guess the original idea started when I was at college more than 20yrs beforehand, sharing a hostel with thirty other students. We had a communal kitchen with five pans (three sauce, two friers), all of which had seen better days.

My unwitting inspiration was a fellow student who was old well beyond his years (he favoured a cardigan and carpet slippers, and smoked a pipe). Every day he would start cooking his supper at 5.30pm, which would involve putting two sausages in the large frying pan with plenty of fat, some potatoes in one saucepan and some cabbage in another. He cooked his vegetables by the Traditional English Method of drowning and leaching. Some time later, when the sausages had turned black and he was quite sure that the last vestiges of vegetable flavour could be poured down the sink, he'd carefully dish up his meal and eat it reflectively, leaving his dead pans to anyone else who came down. All right, he did his own washing up eventually, but I couldn't help thinking "There must be a better way than that".

I called it *Jette Cuisine* as a snappy title for fast tasty cooking. *Jette* because it sounds like "Jet", but is actually French for "Throw"; *Cuisine* is synonymous with good cooking, but is also French for "Kitchen". (For those of us untroubled by a knowledge of French, pronounce it "Zhett Quiz-een", the "J" is a soft "Z" as in "Zsa-Zsa"; I'm sorry to labour the point, but it's always helpful to kick off in the right direction.) So as well as being fast cooking, it's informal (just throw it in), and it covers more than just the cooking, everything in the kitchen – even the washing up is fast!

That's the ideal. And how do we get to it? Here are the Rules (there are 10 of them, as in all the Best Books):
1. **Don't be ruled by the Rules.** This first general rule applies to much more than just *Jette Cuisine*, but is fundamental. If the rules get in the way, bend them. Be their master, not their slave.
2. **Food tastes better cooked together.** Two matched ingredients taste better cooked together than cooked separately; they contribute to each other's flavour during the cook.
3. **Don't overcook, quick is better than slow.** Almost any food we buy these days can be eaten raw. Notable exceptions are kidney beans, most meats (particularly chicken), but that's about it. We can always cook a bit more (although it takes a bit longer), but we can't uncook. Less cooking retains more of the goodness and original texture, and you've got a life to lead away from the kitchen.

4. **Prepare as you go.** Don't chop everything up beforehand and arrange it in glass dishes before you switch the cooker on. Start cooking the first ingredients as you prepare the rest.
5. **Slow things first.** Start by cooking the potatoes and add the mushrooms at the end, they'll end up cooked together. (The other way round we'd have raw spuds in black water – OK if you like that sort of thing.)
6. **Don't throw anything away.** If it was good enough to buy, it's good enough not to waste. Kidney beans (cooking water thereof) is an exception to this one as well.
7. **Don't use two pans where one will do.** This is a combination of Rules 2 & 6: the more pans we use, the more waste we get. It also saves on washing up.
8. **Don't be conventional.** If you think peanuts and marmalade go together, go for it. Listen to other opinion if you will, but don't be put off.
9. **Serve with confidence.** You've cooked it, so don't let anyone else tell you how it should have turned out.
10. **Keep it simple.** There's always an easy way, so keep looking for it. If things start getting complicated – and slow – ask yourself what you're getting out of the extra effort. If in doubt, cut it out.

That's it. I'm sorry that half the Rules are negatives: it's much better to be positive. But even these negatives are releases: they make life easier and the food taste better.

Don't try to memorise all these Rules parrot-fashion; I certainly don't. But do put them all together to form a picture in your mind of what *Jette Cuisine* is about; then memorise that picture. And colour it in to your own taste.

We could summarise the above by calling it "One Pot Cooking". But that covers stews and casseroles which are slow cooking. Although we don't actually watch a casserole for three hours, we lose the distinction of the different ingredients during that time, the variety of textures, the ease of washing up, and where's the gain in the extra time?

To get the full benefit of *Jette Cuisine*, I use a different form of cooking which is so simple I can't understand why it's not more widely known. Unless everyone thinks it's so simple they don't bother to describe it. There isn't even a name for it like "frying" or "roasting"; so what is it?

To get there, let's back-track to understand the three main methods of cooking on a hob: Boiling, Steaming and Frying.

Boiling is the coolest method of the three. And cooking, like any chemical reaction, is quicker the hotter it is. So boiling is the slowest method. It is also the cornerstone of the Great English Vegetable Massacre. We fill a pan with water and bring it to the boil; it can get no hotter than 100°C (unless it's in a pressure cooker). We put in our ingredients so that they are covered by the boiling water, and the ingredients share their flavour with the boiling water as they cook. If we then throw away the water, we throw away the taste. Boiling is slow (and wasteful of fuel), partly because of the time it takes to heat up all that water. So, unless we're cooking food like pasta or rice that need to absorb water to cook, or we're making soup, DON'T BOIL ANYTHING: who needs to go to such trouble to lose so much flavour?

Steaming is the next hottest after boiling. Steam has to be hotter than 100°C, so steaming cooks quicker than boiling. We put a small amount of water into our pan, bring it to the boil with the lid on, and cook our ingredients in the steam above the water. The steam condenses back into small water droplets on the ingredients during cooking, taking some flavour back down into the boiling water; but not nearly so much as with boiling because the ingredients aren't surrounded by water sloshing about, and, being quicker, there's less time to lose the flavour. A good healthy method of cooking (no fat). Drawbacks are that there's a lot of associated paraphernalia (have you ever seen proper kitchen steamers?) with baskets, sometimes bamboo (for Chinese *Dim Sum*), all of which makes clearing up afterwards a bit labour-intensive. And what do we do with that little bit of liquid at the bottom that's full of flavour? If it boils dry, we end up with a disaster on our hands.

Frying is the hottest and fastest of all. A lot depends on the fat or oil we use: different oils cook at different temperatures. I use olive oil because it's healthy (for an oil), and cooks at a high temperature; whereas margarine (for example) would give about the coolest frying we could get. Most of our ingredients (meat, vegetables) contain water, which wants to boil off when it hits the hot oil: that's the sizzling we get when frying. After this water's gone, the food starts to caramelise outside, which helps to seal the remaining juices inside. If we shallow fry, we have to keep turning the food to get it cooked all round, so the process takes quite a time. Deep frying seals and cooks all round almost instantaneously, but then there's the problem of how to cook the middle without burning the outside. So we tend to put a protective layer (batter) around the food we deep fry, and the food itself cooks sealed in its own little oven. Shallow frying keeps taste in, but is quite slow, labour-intensive, messy (in terms of spatter), and not too healthy with that oil. But not as unhealthy as deep frying, which packs in more fat, and is the single greatest cause of houses burning down. Not that quick either, by the time we've heated all the oil.

So Boiling is slow and tasteless, Steaming is quicker and tasty, but with cumbersome equipment and disaster potential, Frying is unhealthy and messy. So what's the method?

Where possible, I use a combination of shallow frying and steaming. Effectively it's shallow frying with the lid on, but done in a saucepan rather than a frying pan. The chefs sometimes refer to "sweating" onions, which may be much the same thing, but I'm not going to base an entire book around sweating. I could call it "Steam Frying", but straightforward "Zhet" is easier, so let's create the word in

English. I know it sounds the same as *"Jette"*, but it refers only to steam frying, not the whole mullarkey.

Zhetting:
To zhet, we put a very small amount of oil (much less than for shallow frying, perhaps a teaspoonful to you Recipe Buffs) into the saucepan, start heating it, put our food in, and put the lid back on to prevent the food's own steam escaping. We'll normally start with a high heat under the pan to get the steam started, and then reduce the heat right down to keep the steaming gentle (as we get practised, we'll know when to do this by the sound the pan makes, without even having to remove the lid). All we have to do is shake the pan occasionally to make sure the food doesn't get caught at the bottom, the food cooks in its own steam, and that's it.

We end up with food that's been steamed for taste and health, but with the caramelising of frying, and no excess liquid: just a little moist glaze so that we don't have to add any decorative butter afterwards. And we've done it with the speed of steaming, without the risk of burning, leaving only a single pan to wash up.

We may find that we stir-fry towards the end because we've taken the lid off to add our last ingredients. This doesn't matter because we've already got the benefit from zhetting the early ingredients, and the final touches probably add bit of liquid as well, so nothing will dry out.

If you haven't zhetted before, start with some potatoes (see page 38 for more guidance), don't go for a complete meal straight away. I think you'll be surprised at how fast they cook, the wonderful texture and flavour, quite unlike anything you'll get served in a restaurant, much better. It really is that easy, but you'll need to convince yourself by doing it yourself.

We can cook anything by this method: potatoes with Mars bars if that's your bag. Because I see *Jette Cuisine* as a daily method, I will be basing the following chapters on good old "Meat & 2 Veg" ideas, or more broadly a balanced diet of carbohydrate, protein and fruit/vegetables. There'll be a chapter on each of these components.

You'll find no reference to pastry in this book, other than here. This is because I think pastry is the messiest and most time-consuming method of combining ingredients which aren't going to do us any good anyway. And it's easy to get wrong. Nobody serves pastry on its own, it tastes too dull, it's used as edible packing for other ingredients. (In the old days of primitive cookers, pastry was only used to prevent food from burning, and was thrown away afterwards. Why do we eat it now? Progress!) So don't bother with the packing, it's doing you harm, and if you're hungry add more of the ingredients that do you good. No doubt there is a host of pastry chefs out there getting up in arms over this, and why not? Pastry dishes can be very nice, if someone else cooks them. If you want to be that someone, there are already plenty of books telling you how without my getting involved.

The Gain-Line is 10mins. Zhetted potatoes will take about this time to slice and cook (for cheap white spuds, expensive ones take longer), and the meat and veg will be quicker than this, so the whole dish takes about 10mins. The same is true if we use pasta (though some types take longer, see later). If we use rice we'll take longer, with bread we can be even quicker. So 10mins is the typical target to aim for.

We're aiming for a continuous process here: chop our first ingredients and put them in the pan; chop the next, put them in and so on. By the time we've chopped everything and put it in the pan, the meal is cooked. We can't get any quicker than this ideal; see how close to it we can get.

Going back to the start of this Chapter, when I wrote "Quicker than convenience food", no doubt you thought to yourself "Oh Yes?". Oh Yes! Maybe not if your idea of convenience food is a chilled meal slammed in the microwave for two minutes, so that the meat toughens before the vegetables are warm. But by the time we stir it, let it rest, and then try to spoon it out of those flimsy container, my ten minutes is looking more competitive. And it goes into the lead if we are feeding more than one person, if any of us has a larger appetite than a sparrow, if we oven bake instead, or any combination.

Don't worry if it takes longer than 10mins: some foods do. We will still be faster than conventional methods, no slower than convenience food (after all, *Jette Cuisine* is convenience cooking), and have the comfort of knowing what we've put in: no surprise additives. We're in control, no-one else.

So much for the principles of *Jette Cuisine*, now's the time to get stuck in. We'll start with Tools we'll need, and discuss Taste & Texture, before a more detailed look at Carbohydrates, Vegetables and Proteins.

After a quick digression on Health.

HEALTH
We Are What We Do

Jette Cuisine is a powerful method, enabling us to cook any ingredients we want, so here is a little background on why – rightly or wrongly - I suggest the ingredients I do.

By now, even the most absent-minded reader will have noticed that I've got my claws into fat. The Traditional English Cooking brigade have probably binned this book already. They forget that Traditional English Cooking – steak & kidney pudding, spotted dick and other heart-stoppers - was the accompaniment to Traditional English Heating; I can remember scraping the frost off the inside of my bedroom window sufficiently clearly to be not that nostalgic.

In the old days before central heating, our bodies burned off fat just trying to keep warm, and the bit of weight we put on was valuable insulation. It was also a fashion statement: "fat" meant "prosperous". How times have changed.

It's not that I'm against fat: we need some fat in our diet, though not nearly as much as we can easily eat. I love butter and cream (the two fats that immediately spring to mind), so I need to cut out other fats to make room for these. And eat them sparingly. Unnecessary fats are what I'm against, fats that add nothing to a dish, but are there for the food manufacturer's convenience or by the cook's thoughtlessness.

Why do people spread "low-fat" margarine on their bread: is it possible they actually like the taste? If they are sufficiently interested in health to buy "low-fat", why not cut it out altogether? As a child, my parents used to tell me how, in the war, they would have either butter or jam on bread, but not both. At the time that seemed to me to be an almost unspeakable hardship, but now I prefer it that way: I can really enjoy the butter without the distraction of jam. Toast and honey – no grease – is another star turn. Try plain bread from time to time: you'll be surprised how good it tastes, and how it wakes up the taste-buds, particularly if they've been dulled by eating a lot of curry. When we're making sandwiches, there's enough taste in the filling, why spread on grease? Use a little salad cream, ketchup, mustard instead if you want; but cut out the useless fat.

"We are what we eat" is only part of the truth: we are also how much exercise we take. Even this is not the whole truth: we all know people who put on weight regardless of how much they run around, while others will be thin however hard they try. "We are what we are" has a ring of truth to it, but is a waste of words for an empty fatalism, an excuse for doing nothing. That's why I prefer "We are what we do", eating and exercise being part of what we do. Philosophers can discuss this statement for years, but we'll move on.

I firmly believe that good diet and sensible exercise are the keys to health, and that doesn't mean dull food and treadmill sessions. It means food we want to eat that we know isn't doing us harm, and taking care not to be a total couch-potato. I'm going to talk about food from this standpoint, and if you differ, that's OK by me. Take what I say in my context and adapt it to your own.

Plenty of conflicting advice has already been written on diet. I would just say that we have to find what suits us, and then stick with it. Whether we're trying to lose weight, build muscle, or just stay the same, we all have different needs at different times. If we ate exactly the same things all through life, as well as being boring, we wouldn't match our body's needs that change from time to time. So we adapt our tastes accordingly.

Listen to your body: if it needs something, you will tend to want to eat that thing. We have to be careful about this: if our body says "Chocolate!" and we're trying to lose weight (that's the head talking, not the body), don't use it as an excuse to gorge chocolate bars and then wonder why you've put on a few pounds. We have to work through the craving, so that our body gets used to the new rules; then the cravings will go away. If we can actually <u>enjoy</u> frustrating the cravings and feeling it doing us good, that's the best way to work through them. But know when to stop before becoming anorexic. Give yourself treats, but don't let them be chocolate if that's what you're trying to give up. Have some exotic fruit like mango instead, or even an apple.

If you haven't tried this, you'll be surprised how quickly it works. Every time you want chocolate, eat some fresh fruit. On Day 1, you'll still be wanting the chocolate; stick with the fruit. On Day 2, you'll start to feel the benefit of not eating chocolate, cleaner in yourself (but you'll still want chocolate). The urges diminish with time until, by Day 7, the chocolate urge will have gone, you'll wonder how you ever needed it. But this only works if you don't have a single chocolate during these seven days. If you have just one, you're back to Square One.

This works for anything; I give chocolate as an example because it seems to be the principal passion of unsuccessful slimmers. Giving up sugar in coffee is another seven-day wonder, and this one is perhaps the most fundamental aid to slimming: it is such a huge shift away from sweet taste, once we've mastered it, we won't want other sweet things nearly as much.

When we've broken the cravings for things that aren't good for us, we can start treating ourselves to them, just occasionally, and not before. But always keep it under control: it's so easy for it to get out of hand.

Another tip: try starting the day with Fruit Salad from the fridge; make up a week's supply beforehand (and make it substantial rather than watery, see p95). I find that if I start the day eating clean, I want to go on eating clean.

Cut out puddings. They're a whole lot of trouble for very little gain. Make up for them by having bigger main courses, more food without sugar and fat. This fits well with *Jette Cuisine*: the more ingredients we add, the more quantity we make, so it's easy to make one-course meals. Indeed the only problem – yes, the only problem – with *Jette Cuisine* for a single person is that if we're adding lots of ingredients, we may end up with too much for one meal (unless we add half a mushroom or a quarter tomato, and I don't go to that trouble), so we might have to save some for later. There's no excuse for filling up with a pudding. Have a piece of fruit instead; we can serve it up nicely if we're giving a party.

Once we know what we should eat, this book should help you prepare it your own way, without adding other people's ingredients that don't suit you. Eat plenty of it, then go and do something else. That's why I concentrate on vegetables: we can eat just about as many as we like without putting on weight. (How many fat vegetarians do you know?) Make them more interesting and nutritious with meat, fish, cheese as you fancy, but eat plenty vegetables to fill you up.

Don't be pre-occupied with diet, to the extent that you're always thinking of your next meal. If we keep busy through the day, we can easily go without lunch. Most of us in the western world eat far more than we need anyway, so cutting out a meal here and there won't harm us. Does anyone really eat the three-meal-a-day diets they print in the papers running for a week or more, planning so far in advance, surrendering their own needs to the scribblings of an unknown hack? No wonder dieting becomes obsessive.

Many diets are broken out of plain boredom, by people who couldn't think of anything else to do and so made themselves a snack. This wakes up the stomach for the next meal. Go for a little walk instead. I've always found that, as well as stopping me eating the snack I walked out on, exercise makes me less hungry afterwards; so I get the triple bonus of healthy exercise, a snack and half a meal saved.

Have plain meals (like porridge) from time to time, so that you appreciate varied meals the more. At one time I used to eat plain muesli for breakfast and two plain rolls (no filling) for lunch: that kept my body going during the day and I could eat whatever I liked in the evening, which was a real treat. I know that this is unfashionable, that we are supposed to eat a big breakfast, moderate lunch and small supper, but that's never suited me: large meals make me feel sleepy and lethargic, a bit of hunger keeps me alert. But this is about you, not me, so find what suits you and stick to it.

That's the beauty of *Jette Cuisine*: it gives us the confidence to select whatever ingredients we want – or our body needs – and turn them into a meal so delicious we want to eat healthy. We gain control of ourselves, whatever our circumstances, and take it away from the food processors and recipe writers.

If you read all this as prejudice against fat people, you're wrong. It's about healthy eating. Some people will always be big, just as some will always be thin. If this is you, be big and healthy, or thin and healthy: don't bury yourself in comfort foods (which lead to the ultimate discomfort of a heart attack).

Most importantly, be happy with who and what you can be: don't be a pale imitation of someone else.

And that's quite enough of that.

TOOLS
The Spacious Kitchen.

You know the size of your kitchen better than I do. Whatever size it is, don't be tempted to fill it with every gadget you can see. Compared with all the kit that's available in the shops, each with a purpose all its own, you might be surprised how little we really need to cook great food. Here's a shopping list, divided into Essentials, Nice-To-Haves, and Gifts (we'd rather someone else had them).

Essentials

Saucepan. Large and non-stick, with a lid.
Get the largest you (and your cooker) can handle comfortably. This probably means a lightweight pan that it is not the most expensive you can buy, and won't last you a lifetime; not a problem, you'll probably decorate your kitchen or move house more than once, and I trust you have better things than a saucepan to inspire your new décor. Large will enable it to double as a frying pan, and cook large quantities as well as small. You could get a wok, but I find they don't sit properly on a modern hob, and they're too big and heavy, so flat-bottomed suits me fine.

Non-stick because it's much harder to burn the food, and you – or someone you love - are washing up. This is why chefs can't cook vegetables properly: when did you ever see a chef use a non-stick pan? It must be part of the culture, keeping control of the menials and giving them tough washing up, I can't think why else they should ignore 30 year old technology. The non-stick doesn't last forever, but even a scratched non-stick pan washes better than one which was never coated at all.

The lid for zhetting (steam-frying). You can get one with an adjustable vent if you want, but in my experience this only makes the knob more likely to come off, and keeps us guessing whether the vent's open or closed. Take away the guesswork and save your pennies.

Don't buy it because of its colour, because I hope we're not going to display it, you're not buying a set of pans, put it away after use, the colour is a bonus. 8" / 20cm across, straight sides, supermarket special, that's for me. So cheap we can throw it away when it's too worn; or keep it for soup.

Not that £65 pan just for cooking custard which isn't even non-stick! It may last a lifetime (and it may not) but we'll not last long with all that custard.

Spoon. To suit non-stick saucepan.
Should be wooden or plastic to suit the non-stick pan. I use plastic as I have a problem with wooden spoons (fingernails on blackboards, that sort of thing). Have the bowl of the spoon as big as possible (without it becoming unwieldy or overbalancing out of the pan), and stir by lifting the food up and over, not just by whizzing it round and round and turning it into slurry.

Make sure the spoon is comfortable to hold, you'll become well acquainted with it. Preferably one-piece, so that it doesn't have a separate handle or bowl to come loose. Black nylon are the most rugged and forgiving. As with your pan, don't buy for colour.

Chopping Board. Large, easy clean.
You'll be chopping lots of food, you don't need it falling off the edges, so get the board BIG. Plastic is best, it won't wear your knives like glass, and it won't absorb flavours like wood. You could try keeping one side for strong flavours like garlic, but I always find myself using the wrong side, so don't rely on this. Avoid laminates: they'll split and separate after a few washes.

The only problem with a big board is getting our food into the pan. Handy Tip: round up your food on the board under the lid of your pan; then move everything over so that the lid on the board is lined up over the pan. Slide the chopping board out, like a conjuror pulling a tablecloth, and Hey Presto! All the food drops into the pan. Protects you from splashes and steam, and the cooker from mess. Do try this at home!

Knife. Big and comfortable.
The biggest you can handle (not necessarily the biggest a shop can provide) will ultimately be the most comfortable. We all start with a neat little knife that's easy to manoeuvre, but you can't get the leverage, and this makes it tiring. Try it in the shop, make sure the handle suits you. I have a lovely sharp knife at home: particularly the back corner of the blade which sticks into my forefinger, spoiling what could otherwise be my best knife. (My fault, it came free with a set of chopping boards, I didn't try it; at least the boards are fine!)

Get a plain blade, it'll sharpen much better than one with fancy serration (all knives in regular use need sharpening eventually, so we'll need a sharpener as well, though not on Day One). Don't get one of those vicious freezer knives for every day use, your finger tips are too precious.

Tin Opener
This may seem like a cop-out, but there are lots of ingredients which come best tinned (plum tomatoes for one), and we must be able to get to them. Simple hand-held is best unless you're arthritic or have very bad wallpaper.

And, apart from the hob (even just one ring will do), washing up bowl and brush, THAT IS ALL. We can prepare with knife & board, we can cook with pan & spoon, we can open tins. Don't be tempted that anything else is essential.

Nice-To-Haves

Pizza Tray. Large, non-stick.
These are a wonderful invention, and not just for baking pizzas (try roasting vegetables on one). The secret is the large holes in the

bottom, which allow hot air up to the underside, as well as the top, of whatever we're cooking. This means we don't have to turn things over, and they cook in half the time. (If you haven't got an oven, don't bother with this.)

Peeler. Rigid or articulated.
Some people might think this is essential, but I never peel potatoes, so it's not on my first list. I sometimes peel carrots, parsnips, turnips, but we could scrape these with our knife if we don't want to leave the peel on. Peelers come in either rigid or articulated types, and I know of no other kitchen gadget which divides opinion so completely: people who like articulated peelers can't get on with rigid, and vice versa. I prefer articulated because it seems to me that they peel with less waste, but the important thing is for you to know what you prefer and buy accordingly.

Another saucepan.
Although *Jette Cuisine* is largely about one pot cooking, sometimes we may want to get two different textures on the plate: perhaps have separate rice instead of all cooked together as a risottto, to the extent that we're prepared to do the extra washing up. Get another the same as the first saucepan: once you've found your perfect pan, why compromise? The only reason to get a smaller pan is to stack one inside the other, which may be important if your kitchen is small. And sometimes we can't even stack a smaller pan, if we've got the ones with bigger bottoms than tops: simple straight sides are best.

A mixing bowl. With a lid?
We won't want to cook everything we eat: what about salads? So get a good-sized bowl that you can mix in without spilling over the sides. Pretty enough to put straight on the table is good. A lid is good too, because then we can mix by shaking and know we won't spill anything. Unfortunately this tends to mean plastic, which maybe not so pretty on the table, and is harder to wash up. The choice is yours. Get both (a glass salad bowl and a plastic lidded bowl) if your

funds run to it. But again, get them large: you can do more with them, and large is no harder to wash than small.

More hand-tools.
A fish slice is useful to go with the pizza tray. We can use our spoon, but the slice gets under the edges just that bit easier. A masher if you like mashed potatoes, a ladle if you like soup. Get them in the same material as the original spoon that suits you. A small knife to complement your big knife. A bread knife if you don't buy sliced. A carving knife if you have the Sunday Roast. But don't buy clutter for the sake of it.

Another chopping board.
I once chopped pineapple on a clean board that had been used for garlic. I was surprised how good the pineapple tasted, the garlic complemented it quite well, but overall it would have been better without. We can never get strong flavours completely out of a well-used board, and this actually enhances our meat and vegetables. But fruit salad with chilli is another of life's non-essentials, unless you adore mulled wine. So get a separate chopping board for fruit.

A knife sharpener.
Almost an essential, but I'm trying to keep that first list short.

A liquidiser.
If you like soups. Easy to make your own with a liquidiser, so try to find one that's easy to wash up too.

A frying pan.
Not as useful as having the second pan, but it will cook a bit drier, which gives us different texture for a change. And for omlettes.

A microwave oven.
This one only just made it onto the list, and mainly for historic reasons: our first kitchen at home was too small for both an oven and a microwave, so we settled for the biggest microwave (no

combination ovens in those days) we could find. We used it to cook the Sunday Roast and many other things besides. But as time goes by (and now that we have an oven as well) I find less and less use for it. Principally because vegetables cook so slowly, and if we put meat in with them they don't cook at all. If we're going to cook our veg in a pan, we might as well add the meat too. And once we put our food in the microwave, we've lost contact with it, we can't stir it to find out how it's cooking. When it spits, the oven is more awkward to clean than a pan. And even when we stop the microwave, the food goes on cooking afterwards.

For all its faults, the microwave has its own clever tricks, like cooking directly on the plate we're going to eat off. If we cover with cling-wrap, we can stop the flavour spitting out over the walls. So if you've the space and funds, it squeezes onto the list. Get the simplest cheapest one you can: variable power and a timer are all you need. Don't pay extra for fancy programs and buttons that you have to press twenty times in order to make it work: how does the manufacturer know how you like your potato baked? She doesn't!

Gifts

Mixing Bowl
Wait a minute: wasn't this on the Nice To Haves? No, this one is the traditional big earthenware bowl for cake-mixing, which is so huge we have to take out all the things we store in it every time we want to use it, and when we wash it up we find we have to dry everything else up before there's space for it on the draining board. If you like cake that much, buy one from the shop with the money you save from the bowl.

Baking Trays
Isn't it funny how we bang on at our children to eat healthy food, and when it comes to the School Fundraiser, we make them cakes, biscuits and sweets. Why this double-standard? Because we've got the baking trays and tins, so we use them? Why did we get them in

the first place? Maybe it's just tradition of a well-equipped kitchen. So don't have them, then you won't be tempted to use them.

Pestle & Mortar

This does nothing we can't achieve equally well or better with a good knife and chopping board. All it does is give good camera shots and make more washing up.

Garlic Press

Same as Pestle & Mortar, without the good camera shots.

Thermometer

If your food smells OK, it isn't ill.

Grater

There's very little we can do with this that we can't do better by chopping, other than filing our nails. In the same category, avoid the Mandolin at all costs: this oriental instrument (whatever you do, don't play it like a guitar) is a *Hari Kiri* starter kit.

Weighing Scales

Nothing needs quantities measured this accurately. Unless we're making pastry. Which we're not.

Rolling Pin

For kitchen warfare since Punch & Judy. Try conversation instead, not pastry.

Food Processor

Rarely in the history of domestic appliances has so much been spent on such bulky equipment to achieve so little and make so much mess. They have complex shapes to trap our food and make storage impossible, vicious blades to cut our fingers in the washing bowl (and they fill up half the dishwasher). Once we put our ingredients in, we've lost all control over texture. It turns everything into babyfood, which you don't need for yourself if you're reading this, or if you do, save your money for some decent falsers. After we've topped, tailed and peeled our carrots (the processor doesn't do this), we might as well chop them too; we get a better result. I know these things: I bought a food processor myself because I thought something so expensive must serve some useful purpose. Wrong! Now it's stored at the back of the cupboard under the stairs, kept only because, if we got rid, we'd find a use for it.

Deep Frier

So much wasted energy in heating all that oil, so much fat added to the food, so much extra mess having to make batter, so much kitchen towel used in "draining off excess oil", why do people punish themselves so? I can't think of anything – apart from chips – which doesn't taste nicer cooked another way. If you're determined to cook your own chips, then buy a bag from your local chipper (no salt & vinegar) and give them a final 20mins blast in the oven on your non-stick pizza tray. You won't find better anywhere. Without a deep frier, you should save money on your premiums for health and household insurance. You won't of course, but you'll still be the winner.

That's the List. Like The Rules, feel free to differ. If you feel passionately that all cooking should start with a garlic press, or you love gadgets and making them messy, then do your thing. If you don't suffer from such preconceptions, using the List will save you a lot of time, trouble and money. This way you can make even the smallest kitchen spacious.

TASTE & TEXTURE
Why We Eat

This is possibly the most important chapter in the book. It deals with the magical process of translating things in the cupboard at any particular time into what we want to eat on the same day. It is very unlikely that a recipe written down earlier will match both these requirements, unless we have a huge store cupboard. We may be able to predict what we want to eat on shopping day and buy accordingly, but what will we (or those we love) want in three days time?

If we are to eat healthy, our food must be sufficiently delicious, cheap and easy for us to want to eat healthy every day. And it's towards that goal that the rest of this book is written. We are creatures of choice, after all. Even if it's oh-so-simple to prepare, we'll throw it out unless we enjoy the sensation of eating it. And these sensations derive from our own five senses: Sight, Sound, Smell, Touch and Taste. In this case the T's are more important than the S's.

Sight
The appearance of food is quite important, as TV never stops reminding us, but we destroy any shape or pattern before we even put the food in our mouths. The colour remains, so I look to colour rather than shape to satisfy Sight. Nouvelle Cuisine discriminates against blind people, so I concentrate on Touch & Taste.

Sound
Sound is the least important sense in food presentation, unless it's sitar music in a curry house. Apart from steaks served on sizzle plates, and certain breakfast cereals, I can't think of any particularly noisy foods on the plate. We can hear them as we chew, but I've never known anyone choose a meal because they loved the sound it made in the mouth.

Smell

Smell is so closely linked to Taste (supposedly we can't taste anything if we've got a cold) that I'm going to consider it as part of Taste. Only people like professional tasters clearly differentiate between the two as part of the tasting process, and I'm not writing for specialists. For me, smell may entice us towards the food, but taste makes us eat it.

So we're left with Touch (or Texture) and Taste as the two most important senses.

Most of us don't like to eat exactly the same thing every day, although we don't change our likes and dislikes on a daily basis. We seek variety, but within the range of tastes we like. I believe that **most of us will eat anything as long as it falls within our range of acceptable tastes and textures**. So our task is to arrive at these tastes and textures by **using healthy ingredients**.

In order to understand different tastes and textures, and how to combine them, we should examine common examples and categorise them, naming different types. I'll start with Textures, as there are fewer of these, before going on to Tastes. And before I start, I acknowledge that my system is far from perfect. My defence is that I've tried to keep my categories simple and useable rather than make a fully comprehensive academic study. Any system will be imperfect: after all, if we could fully describe taste in words, we wouldn't need to eat. So the system might as well be simple and useful if it's going to be imperfect in any event.

Texture

Texture can be thought of as a continuous spectrum between the extremes of "Dry" and "Wet", or in scientific terms "Solid" and "Liquid". For me, the driest would be a plain biscuit for cheese (funny how these are called "water biscuits"), while the wettest would be water.

For comparison, other dry things would be toast (more flexible) and crisps (the oil makes them seem a bit "wetter"). Flour straight from the packet is dry but it flows a bit like a liquid; not that we'd want to eat it this way. Cooked pasta is flexible: bend it and it springs back; even spaghetti tries to. Fresh bread is soft and recovers its shape more slowly than pasta. Mashed potato stays in whatever shape we put it. Fresh vegetables are crisp but contain liquid. And so on.

I'm not suggesting we categorise different foods this way; but just that we think like this for a few moments, make up our own examples using our favourite foods: we'll see the amazing variety of texture that is available to us from commonly available foods. For example, fresh bread, stale bread, toast, fried bread, breadcrumbs, croutons, all from white bread, before we get on to wholemeal, granary, french and all the rest. So don't be afraid of cooking simple ingredients different ways to arrive at a different texture.

Moving up the wet side from water, we can get more viscous by going to oil and honey, all the way through to jelly (which can be soft or stiff). This brings us to the bottom end of solids: cooked pasta is similar texture to stiff jelly. And I'm not going to get hung up on whether jelly is solid or liquid: I just want to illustrate the continuous texture spectrum from solid to liquid, dry to wet, which might look something like this.

Dry=>					**<=Wet**
Plain Biscuit	Potato	Pasta	Jelly	Treacle	Water

Soup is a parallel category. Although apparently liquid, it is normally a mixture of solid particles suspended in liquid. In the case of potato soup, the particles are very fine; in minestrone, we can identify the individual vegetable pieces. Mushroom or chicken soup would also have distinct pieces of solid, but this time in a thicker (more viscous) liquid. My usual *Jette Cuisine* aims towards solids in bite-sized pieces or smaller, with enough sauce to be succulent, but not enough to spill: right in the middle of solid and liquid, with lots of texture variety in the individual pieces.

We might choose to eat potato either as soup or as crisps. The flavour of both these can be made quite similar, yet we would not find it difficult to choose which to eat in given circumstances. We care deeply about how soggy or crisp our breakfast cereal is, when the milk is put in, before or after the cereal. Lumpy custard or smooth? Perhaps I'm labouring this point, but texture clearly matters to us.

Taste

This is The Big One. A continuous spectrum, as we used for Texture, doesn't work for Taste. Many systems of taste recognition have been written down over the years. I think of one displayed on the wall of a very pleasant highland hotel devoted specifically to whisky tasting. It is a circular chart of about twenty different tastes (I didn't count them all), many of which meant nothing to me (things like "oily" and "phenolic"), and I'm very partial to the occasional dram. Too complicated.

A simple system which works for me – I don't know if it's original or if I've copied it, and I don't care! – is based on Six Savours. To try to help me remember it, they all start with the letter "S". And so that people with a lisp do not feel the least bit disadvantaged, I'm going to introduthe the Thickth Thavourth ath: Thweet, Thour, Thcharp, Thmooth, Thalt and Thpithy. Thith ith a rich dialect, but it'th confuthing my thpell checker, tho I'd better revert to conventional spelling.

The Six Savours don't easily work in a straight line, or even a circle. Perhaps they did once, but now we are so cosmopolitan and eat foods from any part of the world, I can't identify any hard and fast rules. However I do say that we can categorise any taste with a combination of the Six Savours.

Crisp manufacturers understand this very well. Check out the following:

Ready Salted	Salt
Cheese & Onion	Salt & Sour
Salt & Vinegar	Salt & Sharp
Pickled Onion	Sharp & Sour
Smoky Bacon	Salt & Sweet, slight Sour
Roast Chicken	Salt & Spicy, slight Sweet
Barbecue Beef	Salt & Spicy, slight Smooth
Prawn Cocktail	Smooth & Sweet, slight Salt
Tomato Ketchup	Sharp & Sweet, slight Spicy

Maybe your crisp manufacturer is different from mine, but you get the idea. I can envisage the workers sitting with pots of the Six Savours in front of them, spraying unadulterated crisps with the right quantity of each and bagging them in the right colour. I don't suggest for one moment that they do this! But it's a useful analogy to show how, using the Six Savours, we can arrive at almost any taste we want. (Think of your favourite food, and try identifying which Savours it contains.)

There are some apparent links: Sweet & Sour are opposites, as are Sharp & Smooth, while Salt & Spicy can be grouped together. But there are more complex links as well; so I'm going to put them in a Table, list their properties, and see what comes out. (Don't, whatever you do, try to remember the whole Table all at once!)

SWEET	SOUR
Examples: Sugar, honey, syrup. Fruits, from very sweet peaches, grapes, to slightly sweet oranges. Vegetables like carrots and peas. **Properties:** Antidote to Sharp: honey with lemons. Antidote to Salt: peas with bacon. Antidote to Sour: sugar in coffee. Complement to Smooth: bread and jam. Neutral to Spicy: sweet chilli sauce.	**Examples:** Most vegetables contain "sour". Slightly bitter in cabbage, beans, more marked in turnips. Herbs. Tea, coffee, cocoa. **Properties:** Neutral to Smooth: coffee & cream. Neutral to Spicy: vegetable curry. Complement to Sweet: sugar in coffee. Misfit with Sharp: lemons. Complement to Salt: cheese & onion.
SHARP	**SMOOTH**
Examples: Fruit like orange, lemon, tomato, apple (citric acids). Vinegar (acetic acid) in pickles, dressings, wine vinegar. **Properties:** Neutral to Salt: salt & vinegar. Misfit with Sour: lemons. Neutral to Smooth: french dressing. Neutral to Spicy: pickles. Antidote to Sweet: lemons with honey.	**Examples:** Bread, pasta, oil, cream, potato (with a sour hint), eggs. Surprisingly, whisky – when dilute – is a great smoother. **Properties:** Antidote to Spicy: curry & rice. Complement to Sweet: bread & jam. Neutral to Sharp: french dressing. Complement to Salt: bread & cheese. Neutral to Sour: coffee & cream.
SALT	**SPICY**
Examples: Well, er, Salt. Preserved foods like bacon, anything kept in brine. Fish, particularly anchovies and smoked fish. Cheese. **Properties:** Complement to Sour: cheese & onion. Complement to Smooth: bread & cheese. Complement to Spicy: salt & pepper. Misfit with Sweet: salt with jam. Neutral to Sharp: salt & vinegar.	**Examples:** Mustard, pepper, chilli, ginger, etc. Look for other tastes: cinnamon is smooth as well as spicy. **Properties:** Neutral to Sweet: sweet chilli sauce. Neutral to Sharp: pickles. Complement to Salt: salt & pepper. Neutral to Sour: vegetable curry. Complement to Smooth: curry & rice.

Before you complain that my "Properties" are inconsistent, let me explain what I mean by each term:

Antidote: Cancels the effect of what it's mixed with.

Complement: Works with its companion to produce a combined flavour.

Neutral: No effect on its companion, we can still taste both ingredients.

Misfit: Doesn't work, unless we add something else as well.

Looking at these properties, we can see the following:

- We can combine anything with almost anything else, there are very few misfits. And if we do have Sharp and Sour together, we can correct it with Sweet. Pickled onions are almost corrected with pickling spices, easily there with sweet vinegar.
- All the Neutral combinations should be reversible, as both ingredients are unaffected by the combination.
- Not all other combinations are reversible. For example, sweet peas reduce the saltiness of bacon, but you wouldn't normally add salt to your jam sandwich.
- Sweet is the great Antidote, in three out of five combinations.
- Sharp and Spicy are the hardest to disguise, with three out of five Neutrals.
- Salt is the great Complement with three out of five, followed by Sour, Smooth and Spicy with two each.
- Sweet, Smooth and Spicy have no misfits; perhaps that's why we like puddings!

Perhaps my most contentious category is Smooth: you may think this is more of a texture than a taste. But in it we find all the fattening comfort foods like butter, cream and chocolate. We will also find others – pasta, potatoes, bananas – that are not fattening to the same extent. So if we're aiming for the comfort of cream but need to watch the calories, do it with a non-fattening smoothie.

Of course there are tremendous limitations with such a Table. For starters, all herbs and most vegetables are just Sour, with no allowance for the tremendous variety between individuals. And I've no doubt that you will differ with some of my combinations, that a Complement should be a Neutral and so forth. Not to mention the infinite number of combinations using different ingredients from the same groups.

But there is an important up-side to this: **as long as we don't make a deliberate misfit, we can combine any member of one group with any other groups and know that the flavours will work together. We can rely on the flavour subtleties of all our ingredients to work their magic and produce a combination that we wouldn't have dreamed of in the first place.**

If your head is spinning with all this, so's mine: fortunately we're not learning the Table for its own sake. It's a way of thinking about different tastes and combinations that will make more sense when we apply it in later chapters to Building Meals and avoiding Disasters.

So be guided by what's in your cupboard. Pull out some ingredients according to your fancy, and combine them avoiding a Taste Misfit. Chop them up and cook them in such a way that you end up with the Texture you'd like on the day. Serve and Enjoy!

Now come the Chapters on the main ingredients. Carbohydrates first, because they generally take longest to cook, Vegetables, Proteins, and finally Sauces. Then we can have a fully balanced diet, using the same main ingredients from day to day if we want but with a different sauce, or the same sauce with different ingredients, or both. The choice is yours.

CARBOHYDRATES
For Energy

I start with carbohydrates not because they are most important, but because they take longest to cook. So they go in first.

Carbohydrates give us energy. They fill us up and give us comfort – though too much will slow us down. Since we all need energy and comfort, carbohydrates in moderation are a Good Thing. They can be divided into four main categories, which I'll deal with as follows:

- Potatoes
- Pasta
- Rice
- Bread

Potatoes

Never peel potatoes: much of the goodness is in the skin or just under it, and it's so much trouble to get rid. Better buy washed potatoes (I'm afraid to say that I buy medium quality washed potatoes rather than good quality dirty potatoes), it makes so much less mess in the sink.

I have three regular methods for cooking potatoes: zhetted, dry-roasted and mashed. For each, we start off by slicing the potato lengthwise; then lay one half on its flat side, split it in half again and slice it across as thin as we want; repeat for the other potato half. We can slice out the two halves together if we prefer, but laying one half on its flat side makes it nice and stable for fine slicing.

For zhetting, put a little oil (no more than a teaspoon, just enough to stop catching) in our saucepan on the heat, put in the sliced potatoes and the lid on. Heat on high until we hear them start to sizzle, and turn the heat right down, giving the occasional shake. (Keep one hand on the lid while you shake, unless you want them over the cooker, which I've done more times than I care to mention!) They'll take about 10mins like this, and we are allowed to look at them, but keep the lid on as much as possible to keep the steam in. The thinner we slice, the quicker they'll do. A bit of salt and/or pepper to taste – I add salt at the beginning out of habit. And that's it. I aim for them to be on the turn before going floury; they still have a bit of bite to them, but they're way past raw. 10mins should be about right for this. If we want them a little browned on the outside, take the lid off and cook them open for a few final minutes. Cook them longer, they'll start to turn floury, and this absorbs the moisture so they end up drier too, more like mash. So I prefer the shorter cooking time, for texture and moisture. Turn them out, and it's hard to believe how much flavour they have. I was never much of a spud fan until I found this method! Now I can virtually serve them as a vegetable in their own right, not just as filling.

Zhetted, as above, is the basic potato method for one-pot *Jette Cuisine*: then we add vegetables and protein to the potatoes in reverse order of their cooking time. One caution: each time we add a new ingredient, we'll be cooling the potatoes down and stopping them cooking, so bring the pot back up to heat as quickly as possible each time, then turn the heat down to prevent scorching. As we get more in the pot, this cooling effect gets less. We don't <u>have</u> to bring the heat up quickly, but cooking time then becomes a bit longer.

For dry-roasted, we don't slice the potato halves, but cut them into chunks so that they're about as thick as they are wide. We zhet them as above, and meantime turn our oven on high (about 200°C will do). When the potatoes are nearly done, we turn them out onto a non-stick pizza tray and put them into the oven for about 20mins. No extra fat, no oiling of the tray required. Then a minute or so before we want to serve, loosen them from the tray with a fish-slice, turning them over and give them a final blast in the oven. Then turn them out, they're like miniature roast potatoes, or up-market chips, but cooked with virtually no oil: just the few drops we added to start the zhet. We can use these to accompany anything that suits chips or roast potatoes. I use them with steaks, meat or fish.

The traditional way of cooking mashed potatoes is to boil them, then throw the water away and add milk, butter, cream or other liquor before mashing. Remember Rule 6, we don't want to throw so much taste away. So slice the potatoes as for zhetting (the thinner they slice, the quicker they cook), put them in the pan and shake them down level, then add just enough water to cover them, no more. Boil them up with the lid on the pan and cook them till they're soft enough to mash; this'll take perhaps 15mins. Then just mash all the cooking water into the potatoes, and we end up with soft moist mash with no lost flavour. Add a little seasoning if you want, and a knob of butter mashed in is nice but completely unnecessary! You'll notice that we mashed all the potato skins in as well: this helps to add flavour and texture. (If you want mash that's absolutely bland, then a packet is best.) But it does mean that the mash is not absolutely white. If this is important to you, add some cosmetic dried milk, which will whiten it up nicely and add a little smoothness to the taste as well.

For extra flavour, we can combine our mash with other vegetables. Broccoli is quite astonishingly good for this: equal quantities of broccoli and potatoes, boil the sliced broccoli stalks with the potatoes, add the florets towards the end, then mash it all together. The combination seems to remove any bitterness from the broccoli, while adding more flavour and colour (like chopped parsley) to the potatoes; one of those combinations where the whole is more than the sum of its parts. Try it with carrots, onions, or cauliflower as well. Or stir in some peas. Whatever you fancy.

So there we have three methods of cooking potatoes: zhetted for one-pot cooking, mashed for when we're using a second pan (or serving with something cold), and dry-roasted when we use the oven – particularly if the oven is already on for something else.

Pasta
It's Rule 6 again: why do chefs insist on boiling up 85gallons of water in order to cook a handful of pasta, and then pour it down the

sink? It may be very effective in ensuring the chef's sink is clean round the bend – and more besides – but it's utterly wasteful. So pasta contains a bit of starch: cheffy gets rid of that and then adds other sauces and thickeners to compensate for what he's (she's) taken out.

Try it instead the same way as we cooked the mash: add just sufficient boiling water to cover the pasta, give it a quick stir to separate the pasta pieces, then put the lid on and cook the pasta with a slow heat. After 10mins, the pasta will have absorbed the water and be just ready to eat, a little *al dente*, not flaccid. No draining and rinsing required. If we want to serve it on its own, we could add a little butter or olive oil, herbs and seasoning at this stage; but we can do better.

Once we've got our pasta on the boil, start to add other ingredients like onion, carrot, broccoli, salami, Italian herbs, smoked sausage, garlic, mushrooms, keeping the boil going to cook the pasta. Try adding a tin of tomatoes: if we press the lid down into the tin (careful: not in your Sunday Best!) we can squeeze the juice out of the tomatoes and add it to the water. Slice out the tomatoes and add them at the end. Leave the pasta in the boiling water at the bottom of the pan, and add other ingredients on top so that they steam initially. As they cook they'll produce more liquid which will feed the pasta. Now we've got a one-pot meat-veg-&-pasta dish cooked in a little water with no added fat. We can finish it by stirring in some chopped hard cheese (eg cheddar) just so that it melts in and thickens the juice.

All right, all right: I know we can't cook long spaghetti this way (I think); it needs the room in plenty of water to get flexible without sticking to itself. But come to think of it, since we're cooking something which is deliberately difficult to eat, I suppose there's a certain justice in its being awkward to cook as well. I wouldn't attempt this method with lasagne either, and I'm sure neither would you! Pasta sheets are ideal for oven baking where they can cook without being moved, not for stirring in a pan.

Otherwise just about any pasta is excellent cooked this way. I normally use twists (*fusili*) or quills (*penne*) as they cook quickest, and are readily available at the bargain basement end of the market. Twists don't have the long lines of contact that we get between quills, so they separate more easily. Other shapes, like shells or bow-ties, seem to me to take a bit longer to cook all through. And whole-grain brown pasta takes that little bit longer than basic white pasta.

On the whole, I don't buy into the idea of different pasta shapes "holding" different sauces better. Perhaps it would be the case if we were adding our sauce afterwards; but since we're cooking the pasta in the sauce it doesn't apply.

I've assumed throughout that we are cooking dried pasta rather than fresh: I've never seen the case for buying something more expensive with a limited shelf life instead of the basic staple that lasts indefinitely, especially when we're going to drown it in other flavours afterwards. But if you find fresh pasta tastes that bit nicer, try cooking it "with its sauce" along the above lines: the arguments against throwing any of the good taste away should still apply.

Rice

The basic *Jette Cusine* method for cooking rice is the same as for pasta: we add just enough water to cover the rice in the bottom of the pan, bring it to the boil and steam it with the lid on. For plain rice, we serve it once it has absorbed all the water; otherwise we add the ingredients as we did with the pasta.

Two principal differences when cooking rice:
  a) Rice takes longer than pasta, more like 20mins instead of 10mins, although we can get quicker-cooking varieties.

b) Rice likes to be left undisturbed during the cooking, particularly towards the end, to protect the grain structure (whereas pasta likes to be stirred). So if we're adding other ingredients during the cook, plan to lay them on top of the rice so that they cook in the steam. Then we lift the rice gently over them to stir in at the end.

Rice particles are smaller than pasta, so they have more surface area, and soak up sauces better than pasta. Rice doesn't have space between pieces that pasta (with its complex shapes) has; so sauces for rice can be thinner than those for pasta. Rice will also work with thick sauces, but we need more sauce than for pasta because rice is more absorbent.

This is one reason why rice is served on its own more often than pasta: it takes a lot of sauce to change its texture, whereas pasta can be transformed with little added sauce. But we don't have to serve the rice absolutely plain: it's very simple and effective to add some flavouring to the cooking water, which is then absorbed into the rice. A few drops of chilli sauce, for example, are excellent: this introduces a little heat and flavour to the rice without dominating it.

We can cook vegetables and meat in the rice and serve the dish "dry" as a *pilaf*, or "wet" as a *risotto* or *paella*. Use rice to convert thin soup into broth: generally this would be pre-cooked leftover rice, added to achieve our preferred consistency.

Otherwise, we can treat rice and pasta much the same. Overall, rice is more versatile, but pasta allows greater texture variety in one-pot dishes. And it cooks quicker!

Bread

Almost everyone keeps bread in the house, it's one of the few ingredients that we buy as a matter of course. Yet we scarcely ever use it in cooking, I don't know why. Bread Sauce. Bread-&-Butter Pudding. Croutons. And that's about it. If we avoid heavy puddings, that leaves us with oily cubes as a soup garnish, unless it's Christmas Day. So this staple ingredient is seriously under-utilised, particularly when we consider that bread which is no longer absolutely fresh is still suitable - better even - for cooking.

We wouldn't normally add bread to our cooking for taste alone. In fact it has very little flavour itself. We add it for bulk, and most importantly for texture. We already started on this in the section on Texture: moist, dry, toasted, fried, slices, crumbs, croutons, bread is so versatile. The best rule is to keep it clear of liquids, unless we want it to absorb them and do the bread sauce trick by becoming a mashed potato substitute. It's most effective as a crisp contrast to the rest of the dish. We can do this either by frying or by toasting. Frying is more durable, but adds those extra calories which we may or may not want. One slice per person is the most we'd normally need. Slice it into strips, then into cubes, and fry it in a little oil. Olive oil is my favourite, extra virgin if we want the bread to taste rather than blend into the background.

But for me, the best fried-bread trick is with a pan of sausages. Cook these slowly with absolutely minimal added fat and they won't burst, they'll make plenty of fat of their own. If you like this fat (I'm afraid I do), add a cubed slice of bread about 5mins before finish. Lift the sausages onto the bread cubes so that they drain down; the bread cubes clean the pan. Lifting the sausages clear of the grease gives the effect of grilling without the mess of a burned-on grill, and we get the best tasting fried bread of all time. Serve "grilled" sausages to those with a conscience, sausages and fried bread to those without.

This works with the fat from bacon or burgers as well.

Let's imagine we've cooked some meat and vegetables and have ended up with more liquid than we know what to do with. Take a couple of slices of bread, slice them lengthways and crossways to get cubes and add these to the pot just before serving; this will pull out all the excess liquid so that we don't have to resort to eating with a spoon. These soft bread pieces will feel like little dumplings scattered through the food. If we want a little more bite to the texture, toast the bread slices before cubing them. We just need to remember to add these at the end, unless we want to lose them into the dish. Or, we could serve on a slice of toast (like good-old beans-on-toast) to absorb the liquid. If we're going to eat one-handed, better to cube the bread, whereas the slice may be better if we want presentation for a formal sit-down affair. These are cheap and easy ways to fine-tune a meal before serving, so make use of them: simple isn't wrong!

In general, I think that using bread-crumbs is about the dullest way to cook with bread, as well as the most labour-intensive (OK so you're determined to use that food processor!) If we want "mash" texture, we can get this with untoasted bread cubes: just cook them for a bit longer to lose the individual pieces.

To Finish:
We've covered the four basic carbohydrates, with cooking times varying between about 45mins (for dry-roasted potatoes) and a few seconds (for bread-cubes). We find that potatoes and bread are most versatile for texture, varying between mushy and crisp.

Rice and pasta also behave as a pair: not much variety in texture, but great for sauces. They hold their texture in a sauce better than potatoes and bread, and have an indefinite shelf-life. Rice is more absorbent than pasta, and takes longer to cook, but is more versatile. Pasta comes in more different shapes and sizes. Try them both slightly under-done ("*al dente*"), as they have a little more bite to the texture; and take a little less time to cook.

Ultimately, all four are about adding bulk and texture to the other ingredients. And curiously, the most versatile of all, and the one that requires least cooking, is the one we cook with least: bread.

VEGETABLES
For Goodness Sake

Vegetables go in after carbohydrates, so here they are.

Vegetables give us vitamins and minerals we need for good health. In quantity, they fill us up without building fat. There was a Government promotion about eating at least five portions of vegetables a day. No guidance about how to make it enjoyable (although they did show a picture of a plateful of Typical English Vegetables, ugh! Was this what is coyly known as a "Serving Suggestion"?). And why only five? Vegetables are the one food type that we can eat in almost any quantity, knowing they will do us a lot of good and very little harm.

So this chapter is about cooking vegetables in such a way that we want to eat plenty of them. And a first step towards this is to make them as unlike traditional vegetables as possible, by cooking them together.

I first became aware of this in France when I was served with a *"jardinère"* of vegetables. I was struck by the imagery (from *jardin*=garden) of a "garden of vegetables" on my plate, not just one; and that they'd been grown lovingly in a garden, not farmed in a field. In fact, the jardinère turned out to be a mixture of peas and carrots, still wet with cooking stock, more delicious than separate peas and carrots would have been. Each had contributed to the other.

Consider for a moment the range of possibilities with combining these two most accessible vegetables. Imagine a dish of peas on their own. Imagine a dish of carrots. Now imagine them cooked together half-&-half. Imagine your bowl of carrots garnished with peas (like a parsley garnish). Imagine the opposite: peas garnished with a little finely chopped carrot. Try to visualise how the taste and texture of each contributes to the other, how different is the end result of each mix.

Already we have five different vegetable dishes, even before trying different mixes (3 parts carrots to 1 part peas etc), or different ways of chopping the carrots (I don't suggest chopping the peas!). We could slice the carrots into thick or thin discs, cut them longitudinally into strips (thick or thin), shred them, leave them whole, each carrot cut into two or three pieces, and so on. We can have thick and thin carrots cooked the same time to give two different textures in the dish; we could add finely chopped carrots at the last minute so that they're raw and just brought up to heat.

As a result of this little exercise, we've ended up with at least ten different dishes based on two different ingredients, and there was very little we could do with the peas to add variety. For now I've only thought in terms of zhetting: other methods such as roasting or serving cold gives us even more possibilities. Now imagine how much more variety we can introduce by including choice from all the other vegetables available to us. Having gone through this process, how can anyone still think that vegetables are dull?

With this range of choice, it would obviously be ridiculous –and tedious – for me to list all the ways we can prepare vegetables. You'll choose which you want at any time. Instead I'll categorise vegetables into different groups (hard, medium & soft) so that at least we know what order to cook them in. I could describe them in this order as well, but there are so many it'll be easier to reference if I list them alphabetically. To finish this chapter, I'll give a few tips on combinations that I find work well together, referring back to the Taste Table so that we can start to see the reasons why.

Hard, Medium and Soft
We cook vegetables to soften them and make them easier to eat. (Unlike proteins such as eggs which get harder the longer we cook them.) And we can tell how long a vegetable takes to cook as soon as we start to chop it up: by how hard it is.

Hard vegetables take the longest time to cook, and include root vegetables like carrot, turnip, parsnip, stalks of cauliflower and broccoli, cauliflower florets. These are harder even than potatoes when raw, so we might put these in first before the potatoes. I generally counteract this is by chopping hard vegetables finer, so that my carbohydrate still goes in first - but not always! Either way, assuming we're zhetting to cook in about 10mins, the hard vegetables go in at the start.

Medium vegetables include onions, leeks, cabbage, celery, all the big tasters. Chopped fairly finely, I add these with about 5mins to go in order to retain a bit of crispness, earlier if I want them rendered down a bit. Beans (dwarf, runner and broad) and broccoli florets come into this category as well; I'd tend to add these after the onions or cabbage because I like them not too soggy, so with 5mins or less to go.

Soft vegetables include courgettes, tomatoes and mushrooms. We can add these with 2mins to go: 1min to bring them up to heat, another to cook them through. One thing: they all contain a lot of water, which can take us by surprise and swamp the cooking. Three ways round this are:
1. Use this liquid to moisten the whole dish, if it was a bit dry.
2. Leave the lid off in the final stages, to boil off the excess liquid.
3. Add at the last minute, so the soft vegetables are only brought up to heat.

I tend to use this third, because it takes least time and retains most texture in the vegetable itself. Larger pieces (eg mushrooms chopped in quarters rather than sliced) help. But using them as a source of moisture for a dry mixture is a good trick too.

Before moving onto the list of different vegetables, there is another cooking rule that everyone knows, even if they don't necessarily recognise it: **the smaller food is chopped, the quicker it cooks**. This is because, every time we chop food, we create new surfaces for the heat to get at, and reduce the amount of food inside each piece that needs cooking. Finely chopped vegetables are easier to eat raw: we wouldn't dream of cooking shredded carrot before eating it in a salad. All in all, a bit of extra time chopping will always be more than repaid in reduced cooking time.

So on to that List. (I'm going to cover salad vegetables like lettuce, tomatoes and cucumber in a separate chapter.) I haven't listed every vegetable we can buy, because I don't know them all or what to do with them. But these are plenty for now.

Artichoke
Comes in two forms: Globe and Jerusalem.
Globe artichokes look like a small green forbear of the porcupine, and are very little use to *Jette Cuisine*. Slightly sweet, they contain a lot of fibrous material from which we extract the flesh with our teeth; I imagine eating a hedge would not be dissimilar. They are best served on their own; very good if you want to humiliate your guests.
Jerusalem artichokes are a root vegetable as unpropitious in appearance as the globe artichoke is in texture. They can be cooked a bit like potatoes, but have a sweet aromatic flavour. Try them roasted in pieces to lose some of the sweetness, or as a sweet mash. I've not yet felt the need to try them in *Jette Cuisine*.

Aubergine
The classic accompaniment to lamb in *Moussaka*. Soft and smooth, with a lot of liquid, and a bit of sweetness. Can have a slight stringy texture, but undercooked are like cotton wool. They come quite large, so tend to take up a lot of the dish; producing all that liquid they can be awkward in *Jette Cuisine*. Not as awkward as they used to be though: they don't have to be sliced, covered in salt and then rinsed to leach out the bitterness any more. I'd categorise them as soft, but I've not found a satisfactory way with them, other than grilled or dry-roasted.

Avocado

Used cold, in salads (see later), mashed with chilli (as *guacamole*), or halved and served with the filling of your choice. Little obvious potential when cooked.

Beans

After those non-starters, beans are a huge group containing some of the most useful and varied vegetables. So many different types, falling into two broad categories of "long" and "round". Long beans include runner beans and french or dwarf beans. Runner beans can have strings along their edges which are best removed, and then need slicing, so they're more trouble than french beans: just snip off the top and we're there. Both can be eaten raw or cooked to distraction, so Medium.

Butter beans, kidney beans, black-eye beans, to name but three round beans, taking varying degrees of soaking and boiling before adding to *Jette Cuisine*. We can add our other vegetables to the boiling beans if we prefer, but throw away the cooking water to play safe, particularly with kidney beans. This process takes very little time if we look ahead, otherwise get them out of a tin, and add them at the end.

Two other round beans stand out: broad beans are a cross-over, a round bean to be treated like a long bean. Cooked Medium, look out for their pronounced bitter taste, so add them sparingly or perhaps serve them separately. And of course baked beans. Add them at the end, like a sauce. More later.

Beetroot

I find it increasingly difficult to find uncooked beetroot. This is perhaps one instance where progress doesn't mean that things get worse. Beetroot naturally comes with a slightly furry skin (a bit like that on a kiwi fruit) that is impossible to get off without making your hands look as though you have bad circulation. It roasts well with its skin on, mind you. It stains everything in its path, which is not necessarily a bad thing if purple is your colour. My mother used to serve beetroot with white sauce poured on top, so there was the excitement of stirring it up to make the sauce go pink.

Uncooked, we'd treat beetroot much as we would carrots, tasting stronger and sweeter, so they go in first as a Hard vegetable. Nowadays we can just slice cooked beetroot in at the end, or add straight to salad. But they still stain everything if we're not careful, so they're about the only vegetable that I suggest adding at the side. Slice and serve as a condiment!

Broccoli

Two vegetables in one: we get the stalks which are Hard, and the florets which are Medium (and I like underdone so they're still crisp). An easy way to separate them is to cut the florets off the stalks (a bit like trimming a hedge) and leave them on a plate (preferably one we're going to eat off). Then slice the stalks into thin strips, and cut the strips across until they're all reduced to little pieces. Put these into the pan with the other hard vegetables and a little oil at the start of cooking. Add the florets shortly before the end: cook them on top in the steam for about a minute without stirring them in if you want to retain their shape.

I used to go to some trouble to leave thin strips of stalk attached to each floret, so that each looked like a miniature broccoli head, but that was more trouble than the above method so I gave it up, though they can be nice like that at dinner parties. Don't throw the stalks away: they're the best bit! Broccoli tastes quite mild but a little sour, so it needs something salt (eg cheese) or sweet (eg carrots) to complement. See also broccoli-mash in the potatoes section (p40): smooth works well too. Try it raw in a salad, adding texture and colour.

Brussels Sprouts

Like a puppy, a sprout is not just for Christmas. Think of it as a "cherry cabbage": same construction but more delicate, and with more intense flavour. That makes them Medium. They're really wasted when boiled whole: try slicing them (as we would an onion) to add almost at the end of cooking. Their flavour is mainly sour, though with a hint of sweetness (again a bit like an onion); perhaps that's why we like them with little rolls of bacon. But they've got enough character to contribute well in *Jette Cuisine*, and the few we'd add at any time don't take long to prepare. Try one finely sliced into a salad (that's if you can find them in summer).

Cabbage

Another huge category: white cabbage, green cabbage, red cabbage, savoy cabbage, spring greens, curly kale etc. They can all be eaten raw, although it's mostly white and red that we use in salads. A bit like broccoli, it's almost two vegetables in one, with the hard stalk and the soft leaves, although with cabbage each leaf has a spine of stalk. So I tend to slice each leaf in half along the stalk before slicing the leaves onto strips. Then add it as a Medium vegetable about half-way through cooking. This is why I tend to peel each leaf off in turn, rather than slicing right across the cabbage leaving a wound across its face. The cabbage keeps much longer in the fridge this way, and the texture changes from outside to inside as we work through it; the outer leaves are harder, while the inner leaves have more flavour.
Like all the brassicas, cabbage is sour, but with quite spicy (hot) tastes as well. Better as a complement to other vegetables than on its own. White cabbage is hotter and less sour, red cabbage is a bit sweeter. Savoy cabbage has that wonderful ribbed texture for "holding a sauce" as the pasta chefs would say; would look nice as a jumper too.

Carrot

A small category for a change: carrots come big or small, organic or not, but they're still just carrots. And they vie with onions for the title of Most Important Vegetable. Really? Consider:
Most of the vegetables we've discussed up to now (and most of those to come) are sour and need something to bring out the best in them. Sweetness, such as in carrots, is the most foolproof way to bring this about. We've relied on carrots as a source of sweetness for years, carrot cake in wartime being one example. It's almost impossible to spoil carrots: even when burnt, their sweetness balances the

caramelising. We're accustomed to young fresh vegetables tasting sweet, and by mixing with carrots we can get the same effect using older tastier vegetables. If it was just sweetness we were after, we could use peas, but there's no scope for subtlety with peas; with carrots we can do as we please.

Conventional carrots: peeled then sliced into discs then boiled. Think again! First don't peel them. I only discovered this recently: I found carrot skin tasted bitter when raw, so I always peeled it off. But I never peel potatoes, so I thought "why?" And I found that once we cook carrot skin it gives out a nutty flavour which improves the overall taste. It certainly makes preparation quicker and less wasteful, particularly if the carrots are little. I still cut off the top where leaves come out, but maybe that's only a matter of time too.

Do we want to make a statement with the carrots or just use them for flavour? Or both? Either way, start by splitting them down the middle, so that they rest flat on the board. If making a feature, cut them into large pieces roughly equal size, whatever shape you like. For flavour, split them again as thin as possible and then chop them into as small pieces as we have patience for. We can use the large regular part of the carrot for our feature pieces, then chop the remainder fine for flavour. Any combination that suits. They are Hard, so add them at the start of cooking to get the most out of their flavour.

Carrots are worth adding for colour, let alone taste. They keep well, are cheap and available year-round; truly a scholar among vegetables!

Cauliflower

I once saw a gadget which was designed to pull out the heart of a cauliflower leaving only the florets; I thought a lot of that, none of it complimentary. Like broccoli, the stalks in cauliflower are a source of taste, and give texture variety with the florets. Unlike broccoli, the stalks and florets take about the same time to cook as each other, and taste much the same as well. Cauliflower is Hard, so stalks (chopped like broccoli stalks) and florets (as big as you care) can all go in together at the start.

Try it raw in salads or with dips. (If you find it a little too hard for this, leave it for a few days and it'll go limp.)

Celery

One of those things my mother used to say had a "funny" taste, so I was excused eating it as a child. This is because, as well as the usual "slightly sour" of many vegetables, it's a bit spicy (peppery). It's naturally crunchy and juicy, and is ideally shaped to scoop dips or hold cottage cheese. Cooked on its own, it loses these attributes and only its funny taste remains.

But for any dish including an onion, finely chop one stick of celery to add spice and texture to the onion base, which makes it a Medium. Go carefully with it (unless you love celery in its own right), a little goes a long way, one bunch of celery will last a number of meals, and add interest to each one.

Or try this: zhet celery with leek (or onion) in equal quantities and a little apple (it's only there for the Sweet and Sharp overlay). Add salt to taste. It's the same idea as a hot *Waldorf Salad*, with the leeks giving it more strength. If you're not a lover of celery, this will surprise and delight you.

Chillies

Not so much a vegetable as a spice, but with wonderful flavour intensity when used well. I don't believe this consists of using so much that we hurt our head on the ceiling, and for this reason I tend to go for the milder types. Some are so mild they are little more than sweet peppers, while others are so hot as to be indescribable, at least for the next couple of days. And they are variable, the red ones are not always the hottest, so try a little when first chopping to check where we are on the thermometer. If they're too mild, use the seeds – the hottest bits - as well.

Be very careful how you chop them: the juices sting sensitive skin like mad. I remember trying to remove my contact lenses some hours after chopping chillies, have already washed my hands a couple of times, and my eyes duly relived the earlier experience of my mouth; not to be repeated. A polythene "handbag" (like the ones we get at the petrol pump) is a useful precaution.

Technically, chillies are soft, so they can be added towards the end of cooking; this keeps their character better focussed. But if we want them diffused more evenly through the dish, just add them earlier.

Corn

Corn on the cob is pretty useless for *Jette Cuisine*: even I am not going to suggest we eat the woolly pole that runs through its centre, and we can't get the corn off without cooking it, so just leave it for sticking those little forks into.

Baby corn is another matter: it can easily be eaten raw, or added at the last stage of cooking, which makes it a Soft, although it's quite crisp. Mild and slightly sweet, it doesn't have enough flavour to affect what's around it, so best to use it as an integral garnish, a taste-texture-colour (it's yellow!) in its own right. Chop it, leave it whole, half-&-half, we can't go wrong – but don't expect miracles either.

Courgette

Courgettes are full of water; the wettest vegetable in this section. So be prepared to lift the lid to boil off the excess, if you like them soft. Or add them at the last stages of pasta, which will absorb some of this liquid. Or slice them thinly and just warm them up (yes, we can eat these raw too, check a slice as we chop to make sure it's not bitter) so that they stay crisp and don't run to water. Or dry-roast them (like dry-roasted potatoes) thinly sliced on a pizza tray, which crisps and caramelises them. Definitely Soft, very mild taste, use mainly for appearance and texture.

Cucumber

See Salads. I know there are recipes for cucumber soup, but I'm not adding to them. Cooked cucumber is like cooked courgette but without the taste.

Garlic

Where would we be without it? A land without breath fresheners, but a dull place nonetheless. Garlic is part of the onion family, and one of the great cholesterol-busters. It deserves eating for this reason alone, but once we acquire a taste for it, there's a temptation to use it as an essential.

I treat it as Soft and add it at the end of cooking: it gives more of a belt that way; add it earlier to be subtle. Twist the clove between your fingers to loosen the skin, then chop it this way and that into tiny pieces. I'm making no further comment on garlic presses and pestle-&-mortars.

Ginger

This follows on so naturally from garlic, and is likewise more a seasoning than a vegetable: I imagine a plateful of root ginger would get us into trouble.

But root ginger is definitely what to go for, the powder is like snuff by comparison. Use it with garlic for the authentic Chinese taste; I'd start with about equal quantities: decide how many cloves of garlic we want and then break off an equivalent amount of root ginger. Once again, the skin isn't worth peeling off, it's like rice paper and the gnarled ginger root makes peeling awkward. Like the garlic, chop it as fine as you can, but add it at the start of cooking: this woody root is Hard.

Leek

I used not to cook with leeks very much: they did't seem to me to do anything that an onion wouldn't do easier. And there can be soil between the layers, so they have to be rinsed carefully lest we grind our teeth.

Unfair: leeks have colour and texture variety that onions don't have; green and white, go as far up the green as you dare. Chop them into discs, they'll quickly separate into rings, use as an onion substitute when making a statement: they don't blend in like onions, they cook quicker (Medium tending to Soft) and they're less tearful. There's more to leeks than being smothered in white sauce.

Lettuce

See Salads. But don't forget we can use it as edible wrapping as well. Fold up your favourite filling in a lettuce leaf for the world's healthiest sandwich (unless it's peanut butter).

Mushroom

There is a certain snobbery in some quarters about mushrooms: we are encouraged to use oyster or shitaki mushrooms, conventional button mushrooms are said to have no taste. Show me someone who says this and I'll show you someone with no tastebuds! Judging by the number of button mushrooms which supermarkets shift compared to other types, I'm not in a minority.

Mushrooms are the ultimate vegetable Soft smoothie: in taste, texture and shape, there's nothing sharp about a mushroom, and no other vegetable quite like them, so they will always contrast. Whole or halved, they retain the smoothness of their shape. This fades as they're sliced, and if chopped finely enough, they can be used just to add taste and bulk.

And water: fresh mushrooms contain a lot of water, which we can use to moisten drier ingredients. Or scarcely cook them if we don't want them soaking wet. Buying older mushrooms that have dried out in the shop gets more mushroom and less water for our money, although I admit to still buying fresh myself.

So add mushrooms at the end to almost any dish to add smoothness and succulence. Whole or sliced, cooked or raw, they are both simple and subtle.

Onion

Onions are the lynch-pin of tasty cooking. Any full-bodied main meal is likely to have chopped onions added at the start; to the extent that I sometimes deliberately leave them out for variety. And quickly return to them for the next meal!

Try to avoid cutting into the onion as you remove the peel, unless you like a good cry; an onion should be a thing of joy! Once peeled, spilt it in half and chop it open-side down; this is more stable and keeps the juices away from your eyes. Buy onions large: then one will normally do, and we end up with less peeling. If removing the peel is your idea of fun, get shallots instead for hours of amusement. Onions are Medium. Add them after any hard vegetables and keep the pan covered, unless aiming to make them brown and caramelised. Once they're brown, it's only a short step to their becoming bitter as well, and keeping them sweated avoids this. All they need is softening, overcooking reduces their taste. Another reason for slicing them small: whole onions require longer cooking, and are a sad reminder of what might have been.

As well as being tasty, onions are one of nature's great cholesterol busters (better than garlic because we eat more of them), so they're very healthy; even deep-fried they do more good than harm, but the less cooked they are the better. The only reason for not eating them would be social, and the best way round that is to serve them to your friends as well.

Parsnip

Parsnips are Hard and quite sweet, rather like carrots, but without the colour and with a more stringy texture. They can be cooked in much the same way, without being peeled, but they're not so versatile: every bit as sweet, but less suited to being eaten raw. I prefer them roasted: they're one of the few vegetables that really benefit from caramelising, which complements their natural sweetness. The best thing about parsnips is that, because they're cooked in their skins and unpalatable raw, they never have to be peeled.

Peas

At last something that doesn't need chopping! Frozen are most convenient: add a whole bag or just a handful at the end of the cook, long enough to unfreeze them and warm them through, so they're Soft. They add sweetness and colour (if you like bright green). Surely we have better things to do nowadays than shell peas, particularly as the freshest ones have already been picked and frozen? Tinned peas have their place if you've no freezer, but they don't have the colour or taste, or the flexibility on quantity, so I'd make space in even the smallest fridge for a bag of frozen peas to keep the ice cubes company.

Then there's mushy peas, a different thing altogether, and *mangetout* if we prefer to eat the pods. Overcooking makes them sad and colourless, so add them at the end. But never be ashamed to serve frozen peas, the ultimate convenience vegetable; because everyone likes them.

My Aunt Euphemia (and not many people have one of those) used to casserole peas in the oven straight from frozen with just a little butter, no water: absolutely delicious, perhaps she invented zhetting forty years ago!

Pepper

Used for colour and (if added last) crispness. They produce quite a bit of water, which we can use to our advantage at the end. They combine freshness and bitterness, particularly the green ones which can be used to balance sweeter veg like carrots and tomatoes, or as a foil to wine and paprika. Red peppers can be used more as a tomato substitute.

Unsurprisingly I never peel them: what's that about, other than making mess and losing valuable texture and roughage?

Prepare them as described later under Fruits & Salads, and treat them as Soft. The closest I've ever got to using them as a main vegetable was when I served pasta with paprika, red and green peppers; otherwise I think of them as a colourful garnish. Even a whole stuffed pepper (the traditional recipe) relies more on the stuffing than the vegetable.

Spinach

Of the great entertainment that is cooking, spinach is the disappearing act. Cram as much as you can into the pan, balance the lid precariously on top, and literally cook it down. Within a minute or so we're left with about 2cm of soggy dark green material with an excellent bitter taste. No wonder Popeye ate his straight from the tin: if she'd had to prepare those quantities, there'd be nothing left of Olive Oyl.

This aptitude for disappearing makes spinach one of the less suitable candidates for *Jette Cuisine*: it's not easy to get significant quantities into a pan already full of other ingredients. Baby spinach is are now widely available in salads, so perhaps this is the way forward: add it raw as a "herb".

Spring Onion

Similar to baby leeks, but need no cooking. Can be used in salads or as a vegetable garnish; a little goes a long way!

Swede

In Scotland these are "Neeps", as in the classic Burns Night supper of "Haggis, Neeps & Tatties". Swedes are a Hard root vegetable, large and round, with distinct sweet and bitter tastes (to me, these are insufficiently coherent to be described as "bittersweet"). Much of the bitterness is in the skin, so I keep my peeler exercised.

I used to find the flavour a little too esoteric to use in *Jette Cuisine*, although they're fine mashed by themselves (a little grainy mustard helps) or roasted with Sunday Lunch. Then I actually tried them, and it was a revelation: all the watery bitterness replaced by a rich sweet smoothness with a hint of spice to keep the interest. So now I'm a convert (though I still peel them).

Tomato

There's so much to say about tomatoes, most of it crops up already elsewhere in this book. Suffice to say they must be the most versatile vegetable (or is it a fruit, I can never remember), possibly the most versatile food of all.

They come raw or tinned, sweet or sour, can be eaten hot or cold, as a sandwich filler or sauce for beans, ketchup. If Sir Walter Raleigh brought us the tomato, we can forgive him the tobacco.

Turnip

Hard, similar in style to swede, but smaller, spicier, less sweetness and more bitter. I'm no expert on turnips, so I only mention them as a caution against their bitterness. One of the few occasions I've come unstuck was when I used turnips in a stew, and I could <u>not</u> get rid of the bitterness whatever else I added. One of my few incurables.

Like swede, I'd cook turnip on its own, probably roasted, and definitely peeled.

Finally, those vegetable combinations:

Peas & Carrots	Sweet	We've talked about these before.
Carrots & Onions	Sweet & Sour	The classic *Jette Cuisine* base.
Peas & Cherry Tomatoes	Sweet & Sharp	Quick to prepare, easy to eat and pretty.
Cabbage & Peas	Sour & Sweet	The peas bring colour and make the cabbage taste younger.
Broccoli & Mashed Potato	Sour & Smooth	The classic mash, pretty and delicious.
Mushroom & Black Olive	Smooth & Sour	A tiny amount of black olive emphasises the mushroom taste and colour.
Onion & Celery	Sour & Spicy	An extra dimension to an onion base.
Peas & Sprouts	Sweet & Sour	As cabbage & peas, but two "rounds" play off each other; no hiding place for the peas here.
Baby Corn & Spring Onion	Sweet & Sour	Raw or warmed, this combination is fresh, crisp and colourful.
Tomato & Courgette	Sour & Smooth	An Italian base, the sour tomatoes make the courgettes taste smooth. Try salad tomatoes as well.
Cauliflower & Leek	Smooth & Sour	Two strong ones, the leeks smooth out the cauliflower; leave green leeks underdone for colour contrast.
Leek, Celery & Apple	Salt & Sour, Sweet & Spicy	Hot *Waldorf Salad*, indescribably delicious. Remember a bit of salt to remind us it's not yet pudding-time.

Some of the above are fine on their own, others depend on extra tastes – notably salt (and notice the fruit creeping in at the end there) – for best effect. By now, we should be able to tell which is which; we're a long way towards freedom from recipes.

And where do we get these missing flavours from? Proteins; they're up next.

Before which (I saved the best 'til last): a tin of baked beans with a tin of chopped tomatoes; each not bad on its own but sublime combined. Or baked beans with chilli sauce. Supermarket specials, no point in spoiling brand-names. Food for the Gods on a budget.

PROTEINS
Strong Words

Meat and fish have traditionally been the centrepiece of our meals: we choose whether to have meat or fish, and then what vegetables to serve with them. A typical bar meal advertises "Roast Beef with Yorkshire Pudding" or "Lasagne served with chips and salad". This is because the traditional method of cooking vegetables has left them so tasteless that we couldn't base a meal round them. They're thrown in as an add-on because we know they're good for us, but only on sufferance.

This should change as we learn how to cook vegetables in different combinations with good texture and their taste left in, but we'll still be looking to proteins for the extra taste dimension, and because we need them for growth.

We can think of proteins in three main categories: meat, fish, and others (including eggs, cheese, nuts, soya and so on). We'll look at these in turn, to get a general understanding of how to make them into a delicious meal with minimum fuss. Clearly this could be an enormous subject: just meat-based recipes would fill an entire book and still leave gaps, with another book for fish, so what's the chance of a single chapter? That's why I'm not going to follow that path: so much information ultimately leads to confusion.

Above all, there's one simple principle: don't try too hard. Cooking proteins makes them go harder, and over-cooking can make them inedible. Less is more: less effort gives more chance of success.

The effect of this hardening during cooking is different for meat, fish and eggs, so we'll look at each in turn. But the result is as described in the previous chapters: we add the proteins after the vegetables. I know this is exactly the opposite of what we've traditionally been brought up to do (and it's not the right method for Roast Sunday Lunch) but it's absolutely right for *Jette Cuisine*.

Meat:

Consider Mince. One of the easiest forms of protein to deal with, we chuck it in the pan and fry it until it's done. How can we tell? Because it's gone brown and it's no longer the soft mush it was to start with, it's got some texture as each little piece of mince has hardened into a tiny lump. We cook mince this way for two reasons: firstly because it's a butcher's by-product containing all sorts of leftovers so we don't know exactly what it contains. More importantly, the butcher has minced all the natural texture out, and we deliberately over-cook it in order to get some texture back in. It'll never be hard, but we can give it some texture by turning it into a collection of hard little lumps, to which we add some sauce to disguise the truth.

Imagine if we treated steak the same way: we'd end up with plank. So this is the first thing to understand: cooking meat makes it tough. I know this flies in the face of everything we've been taught, and it's true that we can make meat tender by stewing it for ages, but that's not what *Jette Cuisine* is about. We know that the meat we bought from the butcher was tender raw, so we cooked it until it was tough? That's why we shouldn't try so hard.

Cooking steak in an open pan or under the grill is very aggressive treatment. Both techniques cook only one side and let the other get cold. The grill allows surplus fat to drain off, making a tremendous mess in the process (if we didn't want the fat we could cut it off beforehand). Neither way is ideal, and yet these are the two normal methods for cooking steak.

This is why, in *Jette Cuisine*, we cook the vegetables first and then add the protein: just as we created a super-heated steam room to steam-fry the vegetables, we can use the same to cook the protein. We've already seen this in beef stir-fry that we can buy pre-mixed with marinade; we can use the same trick with our own ingredients. If we made our own beef stir-fry, we could start with carrot and onion, perhaps some green beans, and when these are nearly cooked add some meat cut into strips. When we stir these in, the moisture in the vegetables prevents the meat from scorching, and the vegetables themselves act as a hot duvet around the meat pieces to cook them evenly. Add some red pepper and/or mushrooms to stop the meat getting too hot and create a bit of moisture, then serve. The meat should be sealed on the outside (which will firm it up) and moist inside with still much the same texture as when we bought it. If we leave it much longer, the meat pieces will harden and lose their succulence.

How big are the meat pieces? About bite-sized: convenient size for eating with a fork; we've already chopped the vegetables, so it'd be a shame to have to use a knife just to eat our meat. How big? About 2cm long (or 1" if you prefer Imperial units; the mathematicians among you will already have noticed that these dimensions aren't the same, but that's the point: they're not meant to be exact, just a guide, so don't invest in measuring callipers). About 1cm thick (or ½") is the most we'd want for quick cooking, and no less than about ½cm (¼") thick to retain texture. Remember that the thinner it is, the faster it cooks, and 1cm thick cooks in much the same time however long or wide it is, within reason. 2cm x 1cm x ½cm pieces contain the same amount as 1cm cubes (and so require the same amount of chopping strokes), but they cook quicker and are more interesting on the fork, so I opt for strips rather than cubes almost very time.

The first time we cook like this it seems like an act of bravado. Then when we taste how tender the meat is and how the meat and vegetable tastes have combined, we understand the benefits. An old rule from chemistry suggests that a 10°C rise in temperature makes a chemical reaction go twice as fast. Following this, meat in juices for two minutes at steam temperature of 100°C absorbs as much flavour as it would for 24hrs in a fridge at 5°C. It can only do this if the juices aren't boiled off and the surfaces aren't sealed so quickly that they can't absorb anything. And the taste-sharing is two-way, the vegetables benefit from the meat in the same way.

Try cooking cheap steak this way. What's the difference between shoulder steak and fillet steak? Apart from the fillet being three times the price of shoulder, we have to be more careful not to overcook shoulder: just let it turn colour, warm it in the veg and it's done. Fillet steak is such gorgeous meat it's almost impossible to spoil, however hard we cook it. That's one reason why chefs love it so much: it doesn't need so much care. The other reason is that everyone knows it's expensive so they can charge expensive. Consider fillet steak & chips, then egg & chips. No self-respecting restaurant would charge less than £15 for the former, or dare more than £5 for the latter. Yet the difference in buy-in prices is £3, for a charge-out difference of at least £10. And fillet steak is easier not to get wrong. That's why we don't find egg & chips at a restaurant.

So try a small piece of cheap steak cut into strips and cooked with the veg at the last minute. If you like it, you'll save yourself a lot of time and money.

The same principal works for offal, such as liver and kidney. Rinse them well before chopping them into bite-sized pieces, which should reflect the character of the original: liver comes in strips, so slice it in strips. It will cook this way in barely a minute, once it's come near the base of the pan. Make sure we've plenty of complementary flavours (such as onion, bacon, wine) in beforehand to balance the liver's bitterness.

Kidneys have the smoothest texture of any meat: round on the outside and smooth through the middle. We can retain this roundness if we chop them into rounded "cubes" rather than slices. And we can add to this effect by adding button mushrooms (or large ones quartered). They take a bit longer to cook than the strips of liver (because they're thicker), but 5mins should be plenty.

I know that some people prefer their meat cooked longer than this, and that's easily done as well. Just be aware that it doesn't have to be that tough to be delicious, and if we don't want it lightly cooked we're faced with a long wait until heavily cooked meat becomes tender again. In this case the best policy is probably to chop the meat even finer so that – a bit like mince – it's edible even when it's hard.

Up to now we've mainly been dealing with beef; before going further it's helpful to make a distinction between Meat and Bird (notice that we eat "Beef & Pork", not "bull & pig", but we're not so squeamish about "Chicken", "Turkey", "Duck", "Pheasant" and the rest, so Meat is animal). The main difference is in how they spend their lives, and hence how their meat is formed, which influences how we cook them.

Meat comes from substantial animals that spend their time walking and standing. They have massive bone structure to support their weight, around which are substantial muscles to move the whole assembly around. There's little incentive for them not to put on as much weight as they can, particularly farmed animals that are not being chased by predators. As they don't run about, they develop a surface layer of fat to keep out the cold; they can also store fat in layers between the muscle. For us, texture of the meat is robust, and the fat is arranged in distinct layers that we can cut out if we want.

It's harder for birds: they need to build up their strength in a way that still allows them to fly, so they must keep their weight down. Their bone structure is lighter and more brittle than for land animals, and their flesh texture is softer. They puff up their feathers to keep warm, so they don't have the same surface fat layer as animals (although water-birds like duck do have a thin surface layer).

If we doubled the size of a bird in all directions, it would get four times as much lift in flight, but unfortunately it would also weigh eight times as much; overall this isn't helpful to the process of flying. Some large birds, notably turkey and ostrich, have long since given up the unequal struggle, but in evolutionary terms this is a very recent thing and their meat is still constructed "for flight".

The end result is that Bird comes in smaller packages than Meat, with the bones in; the flesh is softer with integral fat which can't easily be cut out. The bones make preparation and/or eating more difficult, the flesh can do with longer cooking to give it texture, and it gives out fat during this process.

All of which makes Bird less convenient for *Jette Cuisine* than Meat. Certain parts – such as chicken breast which has little bone or fat – are fine and can be used with vegetables like Meat; unsurprisingly these are also the most expensive. Legs and wings are best cooked separately to let the grease out; they can then be boned and added to the remaining ingredients. All of which adds a lot of time, so while chicken may be lighter than beef, perhaps surprisingly it takes longer to cook.

Fish:
Fish have a much easier time of it: they just float. Admittedly, they may also have to swim huge distances, which is why they have such a beautiful streamlined shape (the Monkfish being a notable exception!) They need plenty of muscle for this swimming, but because the muscle is supported by water all around, they don't need a massive bone structure to transfer the weight of the muscle to the ground below.

The result is soft flesh (pretty well uniform throughout the fish, unlike animals whose flesh can change significantly between different parts) with a very fine bone structure. The flesh can be eaten raw (this is a Japanese thing) but we would normally cook to harden it up and add texture. This can be done by smoking, particularly with oily fish such as mackerel or salmon. The upside is that we get protein in one of its purest forms with little waste; the downside is that the bones are many and small, which adds to the cooking or eating time, or both. Smoking makes both easier as the "cooking" and filleting have both been done. I don't believe smoking makes the fish any healthier (either to it or to us), nor that dyed smoked fish is necessarily any less healthy than undyed (that,

Dear Reader, is a matter for you), but it is doubtless better to eat smoked fish than no fish at all.

In the context of *Jette Cuisine*, fish is harder to manage than meat: the process requires stirring, and fish is so delicate that there is a danger of it being broken down into such small pieces that it loses its identity. To guard against this, we can do two things:
1. Add the fish in large pieces, and avoid stirring where possible. A good version of this is to get the vegetables cooking and then lay the fish on top (and put the lid on) so that it cooks in the steam for the last five minutes. This allows its juices to feed down into the sauce, and the fish can be easily seen for when it's cooked. When cooking fish this way, we should ensure there's enough liquid with the vegetables so that they make steam for the fish and don't boil dry or burn when not stirred. This doesn't mean drowning them: indeed there is probably enough liquid anyway if we've used some soft veg like mushrooms or tomatoes. Maybe we don't mind them burning, caramelising our potatoes for example. Otherwise adding a splash of milk, juice or wine will give us a little extra insurance when we can't stir. The vegetables could be potatoes & onions (like fish pie), peas & green beans (light), tomatoes garlic & mushrooms (Mediterranean), or any variant: different meals, same method.
2. Use smoked fish. This can be laid on top in the piece as above and warmed through for a couple of minutes as it doesn't need cooking; or it can be broken into pieces and stirred in at the last minute: it heats up so quickly this way that there isn't enough stirring to do it any harm. This works particularly well with smoked mackerel or trout. (Smoked haddock is the exception, and is best cooked as if it weren't smoked; the first method above is fine.)

I almost forgot, because it's so obvious: tinned tuna is ideal for *Jette Cuisine*: it needs no cooking, just add it at the end so that it heats up before serving. Don't throw away the brine or oil it comes in though: the brine replaces the salt we might otherwise have added, but adds more tuna flavour as well, and the oil adds flavour and succulence. To my mind, tuna with these liquids strained out tastes very dull indeed, so we would need to be on a very strict regime (or have some very strong sauce) to justify this. Much the same applies to tinned salmon.

We could try other tinned fish like sardines in hot dishes, but they're softer, oilier and stronger tasting than tuna, so they're more use mixed in with salads (of which more later). If we want a hot dish with sardines, we'd need something to balance the oil and flavour: zhetted potatoes are fine for this, and we could mix in some balancing sweetness and colour (like peas) or acidity and colour (like salad tomatoes), or both. Lemon juice is another excellent foil for oily sardines.

So while fish may be trickier than meat, it's by no means impossible.

Others:
I'm not going to spend a lot of time on "specialist" vegetarian products like nuts and soya: there are other people more expert than I am. I find I get to eat plenty of vegetables using *Jette Cuisine* without having to become fully vegetarian. If I had to cook nuts, I'd be inclined to add them at the end, almost as a garnish; if they were the main part of the dish I'd chop them and add them at the start with some onions to try to convert them into a style of mince. I don't know exactly how this would turn out, but it would doubtless be edible. You could probably do better yourself without much thought. For soya, I'd read the instructions on the packet.

Eggs:
Eggs are another matter: so many ways to cook them, most of which I don't know. Three reasons for this:
1. My Better Half is allergic to eggs, so I've tended to avoid using them.
2. One of the attractions of *Jette Cuisine* is that it produces food that is succulent and mobile, with texture. It's ideal fork-food. If we

stir in eggs, they act as a binder and the food loses its mobility and succulence.

3. As I explained at the start, eggs are hard to cook: everyone knows when we get them wrong.

The binding property of eggs is not necessarily a bad thing: omelettes are fine from time to time; we just need to bear in mind that they can get quite heavy with all the other ingredients. Otherwise I've got two cooking suggestions:

1. Take out the uncertainty and hard-boil them, then chop them in at the end as a garnish. If we're going to do this regularly, it's worthwhile having them hard-boiled ready-to-go in the fridge. Do them in batches of about six at a time, as many as will go into your smallest saucepan: we want to be cooking eggs rather than water, and six take no longer than one. When I buy more eggs, I tend to hard-boil all those left over in the fridge. I prick the flat end with a pin set into an old sherry bottle cork (it takes about 2mins to make this gadget that lasts forever) which generally stops them cracking: it releases the air pocket inside that would otherwise crack the shell as it warms up. I boil them for at least 8mins (large eggs), and pencil an "H" on them before putting them back in the fridge (so that I don't have to spin them to find out which is hard-boiled).

2. Poach them on top of vegetables. This method is inspired by poached eggs on spinach, but most other vegetables will do: as long as they've been cooked soft. When we've got a pan of zhetted vegetables almost done, we can remove the lid of the pan and make egg-sized indentations in the top with the back of a spoon. Best at the edge of the pan as it keeps the indentations separate, and each egg will be against the hot pan on one side. Drop an egg in each indentation and put the lid back on, keeping the heat low. The eggs will poach between the pan wall, the hot vegetables and the steam above; the indentation allows the white to spread out a bit to help it cook, but the yolk remains well protected from hardening in the middle. It'll take about a minute (you check, but it's quicker than boiling or poaching), and it

involves no extra fat or pans. Then serve immediately afterwards.

Another difficulty with eggs is the insistence in some quarters that the egg is **really fresh**. There are various methods for this, all of which involve removing the egg from its shell and examining the state of the contents, which I've yet to come to grips with in the supermarket. Obsession with fresh eggs is fine if you keep your own hens or have a friendly neighbourhood chicken farmer, but for all the rest of us it's "Please Mr Supermarket Manager, could you direct me to your really freshest eggs?" "Certainly, you'll find them right at the back of the display with the latest sell-by date, please mess up all my hard work why don't you, and keep well away from the other end of the aisle where the Chinese eggs are guaranteed 1000yrs old." Better to cook them by ways that don't demand absolute freshness. The above methods are fine.

Cheese:

I frequently use cheese to flavour and thicken sauces, as we'll describe in that Chapter. Using it as the main protein source of a meal is little different, we just up the quantity and add it at the end. Cheese & Potato Pie is a good example (except that it's stir-pie): zhet potatoes with onions and any other vegetables that take your fancy, then stir in cheese at the end, enough to provide a thorough goo through the vegetables; it ends up a bit like a cheese fondue. Hard cheese such as cheddar is best, cut into strips (grating isn't necessary), and as soon as it's melted it's ready to serve. This is much quicker - and less trouble – than burning cheese under a grill as a garnish. We don't get that chewy caramelised effect (which may be worth the extra trouble to you): the cheese is melted then served, so we get its full flavour.

As with the sauces, processed cheese such as Edam doesn't melt particularly well, and soft French cheese like Brie gets lost; both these are better eaten raw, save them for salads. Strong blue cheese works though. And we can make the dish with mixed cheeses, put in different parts of the pan and not stirred too much, so that we get the variety with some blending at the edges.

This is another occasion where we really want to be using non-stick pans and not burn it on, as cheese will really grip where it can. Be ready to fill the pan with water after serving to make washing up easier.

Pulses:

One of the principal forms of vegetarian protein, the larger crunchier ones like kidney beans, black-eye beans and chick peas come either as dried-&-raw or tinned-&-cooked., Tinned pulses can be added shortly before serving, just heating them to keep the *al dente* crunch, or they can be cooked longer to make them mushy. The sweetish slightly sticky liquid that accompanies them in the tin is one of the few ingredients I don't feel guilty about throwing away: unless we're very short of water, there are better ways of adding moisture and flavour.

Dried large pulses need a fair bit of boiling, and take longer than our 10min target for *Jette Cuisine.* They benefit from an overnight cold-water soak beforehand, and if we're well enough organised to soak them the night before, we can pre-cook them there and then. I'm rarely in this happy position, but a 15min blast in boiling water will substitute for the overnight soak. **This is the water we throw away**, for kidney beans in particular, we need to leach out the toxins. For me, kidney beans are the critical ones: I've happily cooked chick peas straight through without pouring off the water, to get a more intense flavour, but take guidance from the packet of whichever pulse you're using. If in doubt, drain.

Lentils are the best pulse for *Jette Cuisine,* because they're the smallest and so they take the least time to cook. They need no soaking. I like to add them with the onions so that they get a little frying and steaming; this gets them cooking without their pulling in lots of water, and they retain their shape ("lentil" is French for "lens"). Or we can give them more time in more liquid so that they come out like mash. Once again, less time gives more character to the meal, but that depends on what effect we're looking for.

Sausages:

Don't forget sausages, either pre-cooked (smoked sausage, salami etc) or uncooked. If the latter, we can fry them in a shallow pan, but remember a lid will speed this up and help cook the meat in the middle without burning the skin underneath. This helps them not to burst, and they shouldn't need to be pricked. Don't forget the bread trick (p44), when we add cubed bread towards the end of cooking and mop up all the fat and juices, leaving the sausages as if they'd been grilled magically without burning.

We'll need to be a bit careful about which sausages we cook if we want to save the fat: not surprisingly, the cheapest generally contain most fat, although there's as much variety as there are butchers. But if we're happy that the sausages we've chosen aren't too fatty, we can zhet them in a saucepan, giving the bottom ones a little fry, then rolling them under the others (just by shaking the pan). After a little we can add vegetables, which will cook with the sausages, adding flavour and stopping them burning. This is very much like cooking meat with the veg, except in this case the sausages go in first: they're so soft raw that they can take more cooking, and they'll be thicker because we can't chop them.

We can add a bit of sauce to slow down the cooking even further. This puts a totally different slant on the sausages: instead of their skins being burnt, they retain much of their original colour and the sausage meat cooks much softer. It's slower of course, but we get a better mingling of flavours between the sausages and veg with a much more subtle texture. Everyone should try sausages steamed this way at least once, or they'll never know the treat they're missing!

There are the Principles of Protein; a huge range, cook them any-which-way for variety, keep them underdone for goodness and strength. Always be on the look-out for new methods: my father once forgot to serve my mother her fried egg at breakfast, and in his haste to make amends, it slipped off his serving fork to splashdown in his cup of tea. Of course it was a soft landing, so my father drank the tea and then slid the egg onto his plate where, lightly garnished with tea leaves, he ate it and pronounced it excellent. Whatever the delights of this experience, it was never repeated, due I always assume to its technical difficulty.

Many great advances are the result of such happy accident, and while I wouldn't suggest planning mealtime activities like this, don't be afraid to try new things.

SAUCES
The Cheapest Way to Travel

We can cook the same combination of ingredients – carbohydrate, vegetables, protein – on successive days, but completely change the meal by varying the sauce. This is useful because, unless we buy ingredients in small batches suitable for a single meal (and double our time in the supermarket), we'll have plenty for more than one day. We won't want to leave them until they lose their freshness, so a change in sauce – from Italian to Mexican or Indian for example – is invaluable the next day.

We're all conditioned into associating certain tastes with different countries: tomato & basil takes us to Italy, while curry brings us the sound of the sitar in darkened rooms with heavy-flock wallpaper. Chillies for Mexico, garlic & wine for France, coconut & lime for Thailand, all clues to a particular nation that we find hard to shift. Indeed, Chinese curry doesn't seem quite genuine although it's been around for ages, who knows, maybe longer than in India.

All these national tastes are the result of country cooking being passed down through generations, based on foods that were available locally. They are authentic only because they were largely untouched by external influences. But now we can get any ingredients we want all year round, we don't have to be boxed in by these rules. We always have authentic to fall back on, but we can do better. And this is where the different taste combinations, that we started to look at (rather laboriously) in *Tastes & Textures,* really come into their own.

Nor should we make the sauce separately. It seems to me that the best sauces are an absolutely integral part of the meal, and not added on afterwards around the side (which is only one step up from smacking it out of a bottle). We're not talking about specialist sauces made in their own pan, like *Hollandaise* or *Bernaise.* Nor of instant sauces made up in a jar, though they have their place.

Anything which adds so much liquid that we're tempted towards using a spoon is soup rather than sauce.

I should explain in passing about the variety within *Jette Cuisine* itself. By chopping each ingredient into individual pieces large enough to be identifiable yet small enough to be combined on a fork, we are ensuring each mouthful is different from the next; similar perhaps, but never the same. Compare this with a "traditional" meal of Bangers & Mash, served with peas: although we have three different ingredients on the plate, each of them is consistent; all the peas taste the same, each mouthful of mash is identical, every bite of sausage a repeat of the last. We can combine these on the fork, but essentially we only have the three ingredients to combine. If we add gravy, it's only a fourth. Whereas a *Jette Cuisine* meal, though apparently all one mixture, has more ingredients with the variety built in, without even having to worry about which whether to stack sausage, peas, or mash on our fork for the next mouthful. It's simple to eat as well as to make.

A sauce made separately in its own pan doesn't just create waste and washing up: it has to be dressed to make it look glossy and stand in its own right. This generally means adding thickening (eg flour) and fattening (butter, cream, crème fraiche) which is fine if we can work it off afterwards, but for most of us it ends up around the waist. All for the sake of appearance on the plate and making more work. By comparison, an integral sauce is supported by the main ingredients (rather as a salad dressing is supported by the salad itself), so it doesn't need such artificial aids: it just adds taste and moisture, and it's in the perfect place to do so.

Now that I seem to have ruled out just about everything that is normally regarded as sauce, I should explain what I'm ruling in. Anything that enhances the original ingredients by adding moisture and flavour can be considered to be a sauce. The key word here is "enhance": a good sauce should bring out the best in the other ingredients, rather than just being poured over to change their taste to something else. *Hollandaise* or *Bernaise* may complement the other ingredients by acting as a foil or a counterbalance, but they don't work *with* the other ingredients. The whole should be worth more than the component parts, and for me an integral sauce does this best.

One way to illustrate this is by applying the "chipboard test". Would the sauce have tasted the same if it had been used on chipboard instead of on your chosen ingredients? An example is the chefs who serve delicately flavoured fish dishes with chilli-based sauces that are so strong, the fish might just as well have been substituted by chipboard. Anything that fails the chipboard test does not enhance, is a waste of good ingredients, a three-out-of-ten at best. It has for years been possible to buy a lobster vindaloo in the local curry house. This availability does not mean that this combination is in any way desirable or sensible, it just shows how quickly folk and their money may be parted.

Enough bad examples, give us a good one. The simplest is a combination of zhetted vegetables, which virtually makes its own sauce. We have already talked about how vegetables produce their own moisture and succulence during cooking, as long as we don't boil or rinse the flavours away. If the vegetables have complementary tastes, this moisture will enhance them all, so we have our sauce automatically.

But we don't want to leave it there, the protein will add its own flavour and succulence. Again, all we have to do is to ensure we don't let this moisture boil or burn away and our sauce is further enhanced.

Now we understand the integral sauce our ingredients have produced, we can build on it by adding a few bells and whistles of our own. This is the moment we decide which country we're going to travel to, and add the chilli or whatever accordingly. But why should we want to travel? Why don't we stay at home and make something original from all the different ingredients the world has brought to our door?

And this is where it gets interesting, creative and fun. We don't have to be slaves to the traditions of distant peoples, or obey recipe writers best forgotten. Of course we can use them for clues (and indeed literally), but this is our opportunity to prepare our meal exactly as we like it, not as someone else tells us.

So what are some of these clues? The first come from ourselves, because that's who's being fed. If we like brown sauce with everything, we're looking for a combination sharp, sweet and spicy, together with the base ingredients. If we prefer ketchup, more sweetness and less spice will suit better. If we like all food this way, then any sauce we make can have some of this character, but we needn't limit ourselves to bottled sauce: we can achieve the same effect by mixing any combination of sharp ingredients with sweet ones. (Look in *Salads* later for some unusual sharp-sweet mixes, and see how easy it is to create new ones.) The new combination will have its own character as well, and in creating and tasting it we will expand our own tastes and enjoyment of food.

While most of us have a favourite bottled sauce or condiment, we may prefer others combined with different foods. Certain combinations are standards, and these are the next set of sauce clues: beef & horse-radish sauce, lamb & mint sauce, pork & apple sauce, and so on. Let's take the lamb as an example: the mint serves to lighten the lamb's rich flavour. But maybe we don't want the acidity of a standard mint-&-vinegar sauce, yet the mint by itself tastes too earthy to achieve the full effect. Think of middle eastern yoghourt-&-mint, this gives some sharpness while being milder to digest. Why not borrow a trick from roast pork and get the acidity from apples? This adds a little sweetness with the acidity, which also works well with lamb: redcurrant jelly is an old standard with lamb, roasting with honey & rosemary is another, so sweetness is definitely allowed. We could make the mint sauce with wine instead of vinegar, gaining some smoothness and flavour in the process. Why not go halves vinegar & wine? Saves carrying an expensive bottle of wine vinegar.

Just by following this train of thought with the lamb, we've covered four different mint-based sauces without really trying. There are a dozen other ways to achieve the same effect, depending on what we have in the store cupboard. What if we get rid of the mint and try a different form of acidity, perhaps with a different herb or combination of herbs? Another list of potential sauces, and we only need one for the meal we're preparing.

We end up making the sauce we have ingredients for, coupled with the flavour that grabs us at the time. Does it worry us that no-one's had apple-&-mint sauce with lamb before? Are people so dull that they don't want to taste something original? If the sauce satisfies you the cook, it should satisfy your guests (if not, change the guests and keep the sauce). You have the kudos of having created a new meal rather than regurgitating a tired imitation of someone else's ideas. Whatever the chefs may say, there is no dish so classic that it can't be improved on; a classic dish is generally a dead dish that hasn't had the benefit of modern ingredients, so keep looking for improvements, for simplicity, speed, cheapness and above all flavour.

You'll notice that our mint sauce example avoided fancy foreign ingredients (yoghourt is scarcely fancy and wine is international). Not that there's anything wrong with foreign ingredients, they're one of our richest sources of clues, food we ate on holiday and so on. But there's so much we can do with home-grown ingredients, we shouldn't be fooled into thinking sauces have to be exotic. Or that home-grown equals traditional steak-&-kidney.

Think how mustard brings out the taste in cheese, particularly English mustard just adds heat without upsetting the basic cheese taste; whereas grainy mustard adds an extra taste and texture as well. So have a jar of English and a jar of grainy in the cupboard. But we've not got just two mustards, we've now covered the entire spectrum between them, which we can run back & forth across depending on the proportions in which we mix the two. Ever had honey-&-mustard dressing on salad? Try a little honey with the mustard to sweeten the fire. Better still, try a little jam instead. Jam? Have I gone totally bonkers? Well I'm not suggesting we use a whole jamjar (we're looking for a mustard with a bit of width here, not mustardy jam on toast), but if honey works, why not jam? It's not quite so sweet as honey, is more workable and adds a little bit of fruit acid as a bonus. Put like that, it actually sounds better than honey, and it is. Try it for yourself (remember to keep the mustard in the majority), it has a similar style to sweet pickle.

Thirty years ago, a party of us got into a jam (sorry!) when we lost the mango chutney to go with our curry (it turned up two days later under the front seat of the car). So I made up a substitute from two parts apricot jam to one part Branston Pickle (just the brown juice, I left the crunchy bits behind), and it was indistinguishable from mango chutney. It nearly changed my life.

Don't be afraid to add a little sweetness: new vegetables taste sweeter than old, so add a little sugar, honey, jam, whatever to your old vegetables so that they taste like new (without revealing the source of the sweetness). It's not cheating, it's just being practical.

Jam is one of the great under-utilised resources of the British kitchen. The Chinese have been using it for years (plum jam with crispy duck pancakes), so it's quite respectable. Instant sweetness to correct acidity or sourness, with a hint of fruit, apricot, raspberry, blackcurrant, we can fine-tune the sweetness we add without resorting to bland sugar. What store cupboard doesn't have a nearly-empty pot of jam? Make use! With freedom like this, who needs to cook the same meal week after week?

Once we've thought of the different things we can do based on our local foods and ingredients, we can wheel in the foreign foods,

Italian tomato & basil and all the rest. We can play them straight or we can jazz them up too; whatever we like, we're in charge.

While the simple examples I've used above are essentially condiments, the same freedom can be applied to cooking the meal itself, playing with flavours, making the things we want to eat (or have to eat) taste the way we like them. And if we are to build on the flavours we already have in the main ingredients, we should understand them first before deciding what the sauce will do for us. Then we can look at some typical sauces.

Vegetable dishes give us a combination of sour, sharp and sweet. Choose the correct combination (eg onions for sour, tomatoes for sharp and carrots for sweet) and we've virtually made our own sauce without adding anything else. The protein can be salt, smooth, sour, even a little sweet (think of prawns). The carbohydrate adds little flavour other than a bit of smoothness. So all the sauce has to do is to tune these tastes in the direction we want. And balance the original flavours: if they're mild we don't want a strong sauce, while a mild sauce with strong original flavours is a bit pointless. Lastly, it has to provide the correct moisture; if we've a lot of carbohydrate, the chances are we'll need a fair amount of liquid, whereas plain meat and vegetables will already have produced almost all we need.

This looks quite complicated when it's written out, but it's really just common sense and personal taste: once we know what we're looking for it'll come pretty naturally. Meantime here are various different combinations we can throw at our ingredients to make simple sauces for all occasions.

The easiest way I know to add salt & smooth together is to add cheese. We'll find chefs adding all sorts of fancy foreign cheeses to achieve this (*fetta* and *mozarrella* are currently fashionable) and there's nothing wrong with this, but to my mind cheddar is unbeatable. Remember it comes in two forms: mild and mature. I keep some of each in at all times, supermarket basic, colour-coded, I use orange for mild and white for mature but you can do the other way around or whatever you prefer. Like our two mustards, we get not just two cheeses this way but the whole spectrum between them as well, depending on the quantities in which we mix them. Add them right at the end of cooking so that they don't curdle, don't let them boil. Cut a few thin slices of either (or both), cut them into strips and stir them in until they've melted, then serve. If we boil the cheese it will probably curdle, but it will melt before this happens so that's the time to stop cooking. If the food is very hot, we can cool it by adding chopped salad tomatoes with the cheese. The cheese adds salt, flavour, smoothness and thickening all at once, and takes less than a minute; one of the great tricks.

Some cheeses don't work: processed cheese like *Edam* just goes stringy, like wet plastic bags, when cooked, so this is best left for salads. Soft cheeses like *Brie* or *Camembert* are best melted on top as a garnish, they're too mild for a sauce and get lost. Blue cheese is fine, but the sauce then tastes unmistakably of blue cheese. Cheddar in sauce is surprisingly subtle and easy to use, so make it a mainstay.

For smoothness alone, the simplest thing is to add cream; it's also an expensive way to shorten your life. Another way is to add extra carbohydrate, but if we don't want this bulk, we can get much the same effect by adding yoghurt. Be careful here: most natural yoghurt tastes obviously of YOGHURT, but it is possible to get mild varieties that are indistinguishable from lightly soured cream. So we get the smoothness of cream, a little mild acidity, and none of the associated fat. Like the cheese, be careful not to boil or it may separate, but since this makes it quicker to cook who's complaining? Try stirring it in just before serving, after we've taken the pan off the heat. Don't forget milk and mushrooms either: both of these add smoothness and moisture. Or add a bit of oatmeal; of which more later.

Acidity is about the easiest thing to add, there's so much variety. Two obvious examples are wine (red or white, what colour do we want the sauce?), and tomatoes. We've all seen cheffy pouring a bottle of wine into a saucepan, when its proper place is in the glass. This much wine just makes food taste like punch and hides the ingredients themselves. Wine boxes are excellent here: we can squirt a little (no more than half-a-glass) in with our ingredients and keep the rest for later (food or drink). Even a teaspoonful of wine adds a surprising amount of flavour, so be subtle and drink what you save!

Salad tomatoes chopped in at the end of the cook will make plenty of liquid and add sweetness at the same time. Easier still, use basic Mediterranean plum tomatoes, straight from the tin, no artificial softening or peeling required. For extra texture, remember to squeeze the juice out by pressing down on the lid of the can (as described under Pasta, and wear an apron!), then slice the de-juiced tomatoes to add afterwards. These have more interesting texture than ready-chopped tomatoes, and tinned whole tomatoes are normally cheaper than chopped. But plum tomatoes add sourness, which we can lose with our next classic ingredient.

Orange juice. It serves much the same purpose as lemon or lime juice, but we don't have to attack a raw fruit and mess up our fingers in the process: not very spectacular, but we pour it out of a carton. The cheapest juice is best as it is more acid (more lemony) than freshly-squeezed. And it still adds a little sweetness. It's hard to imagine adding lemon juice to tinned tomaotes, but a little orange juice just gives them a lift and makes them taste of sunshine. (A good trick at breakfast time: instead of adding peppery Worcester Sauce to your tomato juice, blend it with a little orange juice. One part orange to four parts tomato juice is good: we still have recognisable tomato juice but someone just switched the sun on. Not good the other way round, one part tomato to four orange juice, I leave you to pursue this if you will.) So make use of orange juice wherever we want to lose sourness, it can almost always be used to replace or improve on lemon juice, the only exceptions being very light fish dishes or when we're looking for a real belt of acidity.

When it comes to adding spices, most of us think immediately of curry and chilli, but there are many others more subtle, like paprika for Hungarian, or garlic and root ginger for Chinese. Add powdered spices early on in the cook and let them blend with the vegetables to release their full taste; otherwise they taste powdery if added too late. There are so many spices that they're way beyond the scope of this book to cover in full; much better just to try a few and see what we like. But a word of caution: curry and chillies are easy to add, and before we know it we're eating curry every day. This is a bit of a cop-out, much better to make different tastes from store-cupboard ingredients and improve our skills at matching (and correcting) flavours.

Talking of cop-outs, we come finally to the cook-in sauce. Their principal problem (apart from unknown ingredients) is that they swamp the rest of the cooking, there's too much liquid. If there's nothing else in the cupboard or a jar needs eating up, don't be precious, enjoy the cook-in sauce, but maybe only use part of it so that the rest of the meal is still recognisable. If there's a ready-made curry that needs eating, which has plenty of sauce to be soaked up by rice, cook vegetables in with it instead. No rice required, the sauce gets better distributed and isn't left on the plate, and the fats in the sauce are better balanced. I admit: my own curries don't often match a good industrial strength one, so take occasional advantage of bought-in.

What have we learned after all this?
- We can use pre-packed cook-in sauces, or make separate sauces if we want, but there are better simpler ways as well.
- A sauce is just sufficient juice and flavour to enhance the other ingredients, and is most effectively made in the same pan.
- If we don't add too much liquid, we don't have to use fattening thickeners.
- We can use any ingredient we like (even jam) to make sauces, but it's best to add only small quantities of each so that the flavour remains subtle.

- Build a sauce to complement; have the confidence to add other ingredients until the sauce tastes the way you want.

Don't commit yourself to using any of the taste combinations I've suggested, but I hope they show the range of possibilities open to you, to make meals to your own taste. This way you will always have produced something edible, almost always better than you could have bought ready-made, and from time to time you will produce something exceptional which will give you real joy.

It takes us not to Italy or India, but to Infinity, and beyond.

FRUITS & SALADS
Cool

Imagine an even simpler form of *Jette Cuisine*: the same chopping and combining of ingredients, but without the cooking. Imagine Fruits & Salads. Without having to cook, this is the easiest place to start combining tastes.

But what about cooked fruit? Well, there aren't many fruits that taste better when cooked: they lose texture and become pap. Cooked fruit is generally an excuse to get rid of some pastry, and I don't see that as sufficient: we have something simple, delicious and healthy, so why add something time-consuming, messy and debilitating? Of course we should have a balanced diet, but this doesn't mean balancing good with bad. Fruit pies are easy enough to get ready-made at the shop, and if we want to eat pies we're obviously not too concerned about the taste of the fruit.

And while we're on the subject, fruits are the closest I'm going to get to puddings. Anything chocolatey or cakey can be bought much more cheaply ready-made. If we want to show creative flair in this department, pre-slice the cakes or pies and arrange them nicely. Life's too short too do much more, particularly if we eat a lot of them.

So "Fruits & Salads" covers just about anything that can be eaten cold and needs no cooking. And the two merge quite naturally into each other at the edges: we're now familiar with sweet tastes in savoury dishes – pork and apple sauce, the bananas in *Chicken Maryland* – so carrying this over into salads should come as no surprise. Let's start from the savoury end we're familiar with, salads, and we'll move through to fruits. Essentially we're travelling the taste spectrum from savoury to sweet, just as we eat through a meal.

Salads:

Remember how we used to complain that we couldn't get those ugly but beautiful-tasting beef tomatoes in Britain? This was because Brussels Bureaucrats believed that the British housewife would open a pack of four equal-sized tomatoes, plonk one on each plate with four equal-sized slices of ham and call it a salad. (Once again, appearance was everything!) We now have better tasting tomatoes, and this simple dish scrapes into the broadest definition of a salad, but let's be a tad more adventurous.

What do we mean by salad? At its most basic, any mainly vegetable dish eaten cold. Of course it can be garnished with proteins like meat or cheese, but the bulk will be vegetables. And I don't just mean "salad vegetables": there's potato salad, vegetable salad, pasta salad (pasta a vegetable?). The common factor is dressing: we apply a dressing to a salad to make it better (child's joke: why is a salad like a cut finger?).

When we zhet vegetables, they make their own sauce which we can adapt to alter the character of the dish. The sauce isn't separate but incorporated with all the ingredients, not swimming in it but sufficient to make them succulent without their being messy to eat. In salads, the same principle applies, but we call the sauce a "dressing". And just as *Jette Cuisine* sauces are not made separately, so we make our dressings in with the salad.

The principal difference between a *Jette Cuisine* salad and any other is that conventional salads tend to have ingredients arranged separately on the plate: some ham, cheese, lettuce, tomatoes, coleslaw, pickle, all arranged in separate little piles on the plate; perhaps served with some bread on the side. It should come as no surprise by now that the *Jette* salad is pre-mixed as a meal in itself, ideal as fork-food. Not fiddly knife-&-fork style, nor sticky coleslaw: we're aiming for manageable ingredients with just enough liquid for succulence so that we're not gasping for a drink. We'll start with the main ingredients and then move on to the dressings.

This is one of the occasions where more actually is more. Pull out as many ingredients as you care from the fridge and start chopping into bite-sized bits. How many people are we feeding? Take as much of each ingredient as we want to eat ourself, and multiply it by the number of people. Don't worry about being exact: if there's not enough, it's terribly quick to make more; too much, the rest will go in the fridge. But we'll be fine more often than not.

Anything can go in as long as it doesn't need cooking. Pasta and rice are fine if we have some pre-cooked. Maybe we have some leftover veg: sling that in too. Salads are a great opportunity for using up leftovers (as long as they don't have too much sauce): we can always correct the taste with the dressing. Just one caution: if we're in any doubt as to how long the overs have been left, then use them for something hot to kill off any bacteria. Otherwise they're fair game.

Next add the fresh bulk and lightness: this is where chopped lettuce comes into its own. We can eat as much of it as we can hold, and it tends to spring and stop the other ingredients sticking. Use different varieties: iceberg gives crispness without too much flavour, round gives softness, cos for crispness and flavour; mix and match them. Try adding some thinly sliced cabbage – particularly red cabbage for sweetness and colour – for extra crunch.

We could add exotics like rocket, spinach, or that red Italian lettuce that I can't spell, but the danger here is that these will go off unless we're making salads in industrial quantities. We can get exotic by adding herbs to the basics instead. It's much more satisfying than having to throw away half a fridgeful of dying rocket.

How thick to chop? Split all leaves in two with a cut up the stalk, then slice them across the way, perhaps 1cm thick for lettuce, thinner for cabbage. Try different thicknesses until we get the effect we want. Put this lot into the salad bowl, and we've finished with the bulk: on to the interest.

The two basic extras are cucumber and tomatoes. Sliced cucumber doesn't work too well in this type of salad as the slices stick to each other and clog up the mixing. So slice the cucumber thicker than we would for sandwiches, stack the slices on top of each other and cut them into strips.

I nearly always use cherry tomatoes in salads for their flavour, and chop them in half or quarters. We could leave them whole, but then all the juices are locked inside and don't mingle with the other ingredients. This is an important principle of *Jette Cuisine* salads: if we were cooking, the food flavours would leach out in the juices to mingle with each other, but salads are uncooked so we have to rely on chopping to mingle the flavours. We could puree of course, but where's the interest in that? If we're going to chop tomatoes, there's not much difference between cutting a lot of small tomatoes in half or a few large tomatoes into many bits; so follow the flavour: whichever suits your taste and budget.

Try raw carrot, chopped rather than shredded (which goes a bit messy). Only in salads would I suggest peeling carrots as worthwhile: we aren't cooking the slight bitterness out of the peel. But there's so little peel and the carrots are so sweet, this isn't essential.

Baby sweetcorn, chopped or whole. Green beans, cut to manageable lengths (probably no more than about 2"/5cm) for mixability. We could blanch them if we really wanted to make them lose their crunch, and our life more difficult, but that's no gain.

Slice in a couple of mushrooms. I'm inclined to think that raw mushrooms are a bit disappointing compared with cooked, but there are times when we want their smoothness, bulk and lightness in a salad. If this is one of those times, in they go.

Best for salad smoothness are avocados. I find the easiest way to prepare them is to split them in half and remove the stone (by slamming the blade of a sharp knife into it and twisting, now there's something I did learn from a TV chef). Then use a blunt knife to divide the flesh into pieces <u>inside the skin</u>, taking care not to cut through. This allows us to peel and push the avocado pieces into the salad by turning the skin inside out; minimal waste and mess. Or help it out with a spoon.

Chopped sweet peppers add sweetness, colour and crunch. The green ones are more bitter and don't have the colour contrast with lettuce; save them for hot dishes. Red are best: yellow and orange are more delicately flavoured. I find the easiest (and least wasteful) way to prepare them is to cut right round the flesh just below the stalk: then we can lift out the stalk and all the seeds with a little tutu of flesh (which we can easily break away). If we use the tutu flesh first, the rest of the pepper is tidy for slicing, or can be wrapped in cling-film for later: we probably don't need it all now, but we only want to deal with the seeds once. And don't worry too much about the seeds: they're very tasty, it's just the cotton wool they sit in that's best avoided.

As our salad becomes more exotic, we can start to add stronger or more diverse flavours: chop in a few stoned olives; black *or* green generally works better than both together, which tend to detract from each other.

How about some fruit? Raisins or sultanas? Sliced apple? A little chopped orange or apricots? A few grapes? A little fruit here will complement as long as its sweetness doesn't dominate. How much will depend on what dressing we add. Remember that with apple, pear or banana, we'll want to get the dressing on as soon as possible so that they don't discolour.

With all this bland sweetness, we need to get some flavour intensity in. This generally means something salty. We may already have enough with the olives, but ham, cooked bacon, sausage, tuna, anchovy, hard cheese are all good candidates, all chopped into similar small pieces to the other ingredients. The sausage could be salami, the cheese could be blue, for extra bite. We could add hard-boiled egg here, but the salt is the key: the eggs in a classic *Salad Nicoise* are only there to offset the excessive saltiness of the anchovies. Mature cheddar in little strips on its own is my best basic; the others are a bonus.

Dressings:
Now we've got the protein and veg, time for the dressing. And here I must declare my preference: nothing spoils the freshness of a salad so much as smothering it in oil. We might as well put it under the car and drain the sump! We're looking for Sharp tastes to balance the Salt-Sour-Sweet combination we've got, and what does oil do: it gives us Smooth (which we can add with other ingredients), it "holds" the dressing through the salad (there are other ways), it makes the salad look glossy in photos (now we see why it's popular) and it adds lots of unnecessary calories (which rather defeats the point of having salad in the first place).

What about mayonnaise? I finished my mayonnaise phase some years ago: very smooth and superficially delicious, but it just clogs everything up (and not just the salad). If you do like mayonnaise, don't go to the trouble of making your own: it's labour-intensive, likely to go wrong, and mayonnaise manufacturers have invested millions in blending equipment that will outperform anything you or I can do at home. Go for a long walk if you have that much excess time and energy, or take up charity work. Instead, take your favourite bought mayonnaise and personalise it by adding garlic, herbs, mustard, wine, whatever you fancy. That way you'll end up with something really original and better than the bought.

Which just leaves us with vinegar? Not far off. But remember we can also dress with unsweetened fruit juice, wine, or any combination. Yoghurt gives a mild acidity with smoothness: think of yoghurt salads (raithas) in Indian restaurants; except for us there's less yoghurt. We can combine with a little oil, mayonnaise or even (heaven forfend!) good old salad cream, an unfashionable but effective ingredient in the right context. Try a little horse-radish or tartare sauce instead, and dilute it with vinegar or red wine. Grainy mustard does the trick too.

You'll have noticed that most of these ingredients will produce a whitish dressing, so that our salad looks a bit like coleslaw (nothing wrong with that, and we can make our own coleslaw along the same lines). But we may not want this colour, and this is I think the only argument in favour of a classic french dressing: it gives the salad taste and gloss without adding colour. Fine if appearance is that important, and we understand that we sacrifice some taste for it.

What sort of vinegar? Certainly not balsamic, which is, £ for £, about the most pointless ingredient I can think of. We can make up vinegar to any taste we want by adding sweetness, salt, herbs, spices, water, whatever. It may not have the authentic Italian taste of balsamic vinegar; it'll just have the taste we want.

The best vinegar comes free. How so? We all have a favourite brand of pickle, be it onions, gherkins, beetroot, whatever our preference; mine is for a particular brand of sweet pickled onions. The vinegar that comes with these is the perfect basis for dressings, adding Sharpness with other flavours we like.

This is an important principle, going back to our original "Don't Throw Anything Away". If our tuna or olives come in brine, use this instead of salt, whether with the dressing, elsewhere in the meal or saved for later. Because they add much more than Salt, and they come for free. Gherkin vinegar gives us free dill. Caper juice gives an astonishing mix of strong flavours: add with care for best effect.

We dress the salad in the bowl, without wasting a separate dish. Let's assume we're adding a few chopped green olives, sweet pickled onions, grainy mustard: these go in a heap on top of the other salad ingredients. If we pour a little olive brine and some onion vinegar over these, it tends to wash them down into the salad. Then we can stir the remainder in by lifting the salad from the bottom of the bowl up and over (spoon down the side) so that we're lifting and lightening it, not bashing it down. It only takes a couple of turns.

How much dressing? Is it well distributed through the salad? Have we got a puddle at the bottom of the bowl? Taste to see if we need to add more. But if we want to use up the excess at the bottom, we can add a little chopped bread or toast: this will absorb any spare dressing and lift it into the salad – which if we remember was the main function of the oil in the dressing. The bread adds the same smoothness, and turns the salad into a complete meal. Add the bread at the end: we want to get dressing onto the leaves first, and if we add the bread too early it'll just soak up everything. Oat flakes achieve much the same effect without having to be cut up, and they blend through more uniformly than bread pieces.

What to do if the dressing tastes different from what we'd planned? Extra vinegar is easy, but what if we've got too much? We can add Smooth – which tends to mean bulk and we end up with more than we planned - or we can add Sweet, perhaps balanced with a little extra Salt. Don't be afraid to add a bit of extra sweetness: add a tiny bit and taste to see if it's working in the right direction; if not try something else. But this is rare: more often than not we'll get the taste fine first time, even if not exactly as we planned.

We can add sweetness with apple juice if we want more liquid, or sultanas, pineapple, jam(!) or carrot if we've too much. I had a pub salad a while back served with brown pickle and some tinned fruit salad (with the juice strained off) side by side. The latter struck me as a bit weird, and as I toyed with it, I realised the fruit combined perfectly with the brown pickle: the same texture but making it milder and sweeter. Not something I'd have tried at home, but one that exactly follows the Taste principles of Sweet neutralising Sharp and Sour.

Fruit:

Which brings us neatly round to fruit. Personally I like my fruit sweet, and here's a funny thing: sweet things taste less sweet when they're hot. Cool them down and they taste sweet again, so it's a taste thing, nothing to do with the cooking. I'm not aware of any fruit that *has* to be cooked. The fruit gets softened as the boiling juice breaks up its cell structure (the same happens if we freeze it), which gives us the same loss of texture as if we'd used a food processor; and I'm not going through those arguments again!

Even if it's been cooked, I prefer the sweeter taste cold. Cooking makes its texture worse too, so why go to that trouble? We won't. But if we don't cook it, what's different from just putting out a fruit bowl? Fruit Salad.

Some of the most delicious fruit is the hardest to peel: I'm thinking particularly of oranges here: we may fancy an orange but can't be bothered with all the mess that it makes. We may want some more variety than a single piece of fruit gives us, but if we limit ourselves to the fruit bowl approach, an apple an orange and a banana is quite a lot of fruit at one sitting. What to do with the apple core? How to eat a banana in polite society? All these problems are solved by Fruit Salad.

Not tinned fruit salad, where little pieces of bland fruit swim in light syrup. Fruit Salad is a mix of any fruits we have to hand, in whatever quantities we have available, sufficient to fill a good-sized plastic container with a well-sealing lid. Why is it driven by this container? Because once we start getting our fingers messy, we want the effort to be worthwhile, so make as much as we can and keep it in the fridge. The lid seals so that we can mix it by shaking without spilling colourful sticky juice all over the kitchen.

As salads can be used to finish up leftovers, so can Fruit Salad use up fruit that's past its best for eating on its own. We've all thrown fruit away when the only thing wrong with it was that its skin had become a bit wrinkled or bruised. Oranges and satsumas are classic for this: the skin dries out and becomes almost impossible to remove. When this happens, the fruit on the inside is often even tastier than before as the juice has become more concentrated; a pity to throw it away just now! Even if it's dried out altogether, we can add extra orange juice to make up. If an apple is bruised or a peach has a little mould patch, cut out the offending bit and use the rest. Once they're in the Fruit Salad, no one will know the difference.

How do we go about it? First get a new chopping board; not each time, but one we use only for fruit so it has no garlic or chilli on it. Put an orange on its stalk end and cut it in half down to (but not through) the peel; then make a similar cut at right angles. The orange will now open up into four quadrants connected only by the peel. Using this peel connection to help, press the segments out by pushing from the outside to straighten the peel. The flesh springs out surprisingly easily, and with little juice lost. Even if the peel is dry and stiff. Occasionally it breaks, but this is easily overcome. What juice there is goes on the chopping board, and doesn't squirt into our eye as it does when we try peeling politely. Then we put two peeled quadrants next to each other on the board (like half an orange, flat side down), slice across into pieces, and put them into the bowl.

Clementines, mandarins, satsumas can all be dealt with in the same way (even limes, lemons and grapefruit, although these are a bit powerful for most purposes). As many as we want to get rid of, anything we'd be happy to eat raw. Add some extra orange juice out of a carton, and we have a wonderfully fresh Orange Fruit Salad.

We can treat apples and pears much the same way: cut into quadrants (right through this time, I don't believe we're going to peel them) and remove the pieces of core. (If this is for private consumption, the easiest way is to bite the core out and eat it; we get a foretaste of how sweet the fruit is. If we're preparing for a dinner party, we'll use the more conventional knife method!) Then slice the quadrants as we did the oranges and put in with some apple juice for Apple Fruit

Salad. Any apples will do, even cookers (like Bramleys) which need extra thin slicing and benefit from the sweet apple juice. A quick mix straightaway gets juice over the apple pieces and stops them going brown. Or try orange juice for a bit more bite to the flavour (eating apples only!)

Two simple fruit desserts: keep them in their sealed-top container in the fridge and we can dip into them all week as we want. But why stop there? Apples and oranges complement each other beautifully, the apples taking some of the edge off the oranges and making them go further, the oranges cheering up the apples. Try apple fruit salad with orange juice, or orange with apple juice. So much variety with just two basic fruits; like all the ways to combine peas and carrots, simple things like changing quantities, chopping fine and coarse, and we don't have to worry about cooking time.

But why stop there? Add some grapes, preferably seedless, but a little bitter crunch adds more interest and its avoidance is certainly not worth the trouble of individually de-seeding grapes. Cutting them in half is enough effort; the halves don't have to be exact, but cutting gets their juices into circulation. We can leave some grapes whole so that we get some straight flavour as well.

Leave in the wrinkly grapes: they're halfway to being sultanas or alcohol or both, nothing wrong with them. Just don't drive immediately afterwards!

Peaches or nectarines? Just split them around the middle and twist to get the stone out, then chop. Don't peel them! As with the other fruit, use any on their way out rather than the freshest, and just trim out any soft bits. It's amazing how localised such damage can be – and how quickly it appears – so it's a shame to throw out fruit which is 90% good (most of us would be happy with a 90% score ourselves).

We can add melon pieces, but only if we're trying to dilute the salad, which seems a bit pointless to me. Melon is best served in slices on its own. Similarly with pineapple, which involves quite a lot of hard graft and waste: serve it in its own case and make a statement. If we've some left over, in it goes.

Don't forget dried fruit, particularly apricots, raisins and sultanas. Just remember to add some extra juice as they will absorb it and become fat and soft. And that raisins particularly can add a "Christmas Punch" quality to the Fruit Salad, which is an effect we may not want in the height of summer.

And what about the summer fruits themselves? Strawberries are so delicately flavoured they're another best eaten on their own, but any leftovers will add depth to our Fruit Salad. Raspberries are excellent as long as none of our dinner guests have denture problems with the seeds. But the best of all are blackcurrants! I admit my bias here as they grow like fun up here in Scotland, so I have a freezer full of them. They don't need any cooking, although they benefit from a good fester in the Fruit Salad. We can speed the process up by starting them with a quick blast in the microwave (a handful for 1min on high) and then squash them with a spoon to get they're juices going. After a day the Fruit Salad will have shaken into a glorious purple.

Blackcurrants, oranges, apples, all fine strong flavours, but aren't we going to need a bit of sweetness? This is where we add our tin of fruit salad, we knew it would come in handy, the cheapest we can find. Or tinned peaches: there are some real bargains out there. We're really adding them for their syrup, which we can strain out of the tin by carefully pressing the lid down (as we did to de-juice tinned tomatoes). The cheaper the tin, the more syrup we're likely to get, and the fruit is a bonus. But with all our own fruit as well as that in the tin, the quantities are about right, we probably don't need fruit juice as well. The tinned syrup turns our blackcurrants (that we might only have used for jam) into an intense, delicious and unusual pudding that will hold its own at dinner parties. With no cooking! And all that Vitamin C! No colds for us.

So the guideline is: use whatever fruit we need to use up, any others we fancy, and add tinned fruit if we need extra sweetness, or fruit juice if we don't.

There's a difference between salads and Fruit Salad: we make up salads (particularly leaf salads) fresh as we need them, but Fruit Salad benefits from a fester in the fridge. This makes it ideal as a breakfast wake-up (with or without cereals mixed in): it refreshes, sustains, and it's there.

And that's it. *Jette Cuisine* is easy, but Fruits and Salads are easier still. No point in making life difficult!

OAT CUISINE
Simply Irresistible

Oats are the unsung hero of all food. Perhaps because they're local, and cheap, so they have no glamour and are thus virtually never used by chefs. We're starting with quite a recommendation.

Some years ago, there was an advertisement for breakfast muesli which sought to persuade us that it was better than its rivals because it left out the cheap ingredients (camera-shot to sack of oats thrown to one side) and put in more expensive ingredients (various nuts suddenly appear from nowhere). Unfortunately for the advertisers, the healthiest part of the muesli turned out to be the oats they'd thrown out, whereas the nuts they'd left in were full of unnecessary fats and the subject of allergic reactions.

Too late, the advertisers learned the truth the rest of us have known for years: cheap does not necessarily mean unhealthy. Cheap is just a reflection of market forces. And in today's somewhat self-indulgent world, unhealthy food (eg cream) is often most in demand, so healthy food turns out cheaper.

But wait a minute: it may be healthy, but aren't we talking about porridge here? Perhaps so. When I was small, I was lucky in being served a cooked breakfast every day of the week. Except Monday, which was washing day, no time to cook breakfast, so we had cereal; this wasn't good enough in winter (no central heating) so on cold Mondays we had porridge. And I loathed it. I could never escape the impression that it had been concocted in a giant runny nose, and this has stayed with me despite all the tales of powerful Scotsmen who have lived on little else.

My relationship with oats would have been terminal were it not also for flapjacks. These (made with oatflakes, fat and sugar) were, and remain, my favourite biscuits. So how can such a simple product turn into my favourite biscuit and my least favourite breakfast? The main difference is Texture. So how do we prepare oats in ways that we like?

To start with, oats come in two forms: oat-flakes (like paper torn into very small pieces) and oatmeal (hard tiny granules like small seeds). I started with flakes and came to oatmeal later in life, but both can be eaten equally well raw (muesli) or cooked (flapjacks). They absorb liquids and fat. They are filling. They are natural roughage. They have a light slightly nutty taste that complements without dominating. They are Smooth. They work in sweet or savoury dishes. They perform the same thickening function as flour, but with more interesting texture and without that irritating tendency to go lumpy. I can think of no other ingredient so versatile, so healthy, and above all so foolproof.

With versatility comes accessibility: we can use oats at any time and they will always do us good, so the last thing we need is to be stretching into the back of the store-cupboard for a cellophane wrapper which tears apart and flicks its contents all over our clothes and the floor. That's why oats are one of the few ingredients I keep close to hand in glass storage jars, so that they're instantly accessible without mess. Two jars actually: flakes and meal. Just shake a few in, judge it by eye and experience. Little to begin with, we can always add more but they're hard to take back (though they'll do us no harm). Scales are for inconvenience food; we want no recipes here!

And all we can think of to make with this magic ingredient is porridge? So we can grumble about its texture? And indulge in sterile arguments about whether it should be eaten with salt or with sugar? It's time to redress the balance and give the oats their due. They've always been associated with health and vigour ("sowing your wild oats"), so let's capture these qualities and turn them to our advantage.

Any ingredient that takes little or no time to cook has got to be invaluable in time-saving cookery like *Jette Cuisine*. But as they can be eaten hard or soft, wet or dry, sweet or savoury, where to start? I suppose the beginning would be best, so let's look at breakfast and work on through the day.

We could do porridge.

Enough said.

Muesli made of oat-flakes or oatmeal, or a combination, with raisins or sultanas. Mix them up there and then, it's not worth doing beforehand, we can have what we want on the day. This will be smooth-textured, so we can add a toasted oat crunchy cereal to give it some bite. (Or, looking at it the other way, we can add oats to the crunchy cereal to stop it punching holes in the roof of our mouth.) The crunchy cereal is light and tends to go to the top when shaken, so put it in first and add the oats and fruit on top so that they mix better.

We could eat this dry: it's surprisingly palatable. Convention says "add milk". Yoghurt gives us some thickness and a little bite. Best, to my mind, is orange juice. Not so much that it's swimming in the stuff, just sufficient to moisturise and bind it so that it doesn't fall off the spoon. The sharpness of the orange juice and the smoothness of the oats combine perfectly. Try apple juice for the sweet alternative. Or if we're in a savoury mood, mix up some oats with tomato juice and worcester sauce.

The ultimate labour-saving breakfast: shake up the muesli dry in a cup (best half-fill a large cup) and "drink" it. Then slake thirst with orange juice in same cup; this rinses out any remaining oats. Then drink water from same cup to rinse both cup and teeth (dentists tell us that brushing our teeth straight after something acidic is the worst thing we can do for our teeth: we brush away the softened surface). Then dry cup, put away, and clean teeth. The whole process takes a couple of minutes (excluding brushing). Agreed: it'll not replace the lazy Saturday morning brunch, but as a self-starter to kick the body off in the right direction before going to work, it's hard to beat.

Stop honey sliding off toast by sprinkling some oats on top. Oat-flakes are particularly good for this, we can see how they work in creating barriers that the honey has to flow round; the honey can't be bothered, so the mixture "binds". This binding principle applies whenever we add oat-flakes in quantity. Until we cook them soft, when another mechanism comes into play (more later). Adding oats like this cheers up processed white bread no end: if you like brown bread but all that's left is sliced white, you'll know what I mean. The oats give it substance and make it worth eating.

Add oatmeal to the frying pan for easy "grits" in a fried breakfast. Adding oat-flakes at the end of cooking cleans up all the juices (and fat!) onto our plate so that the pan doesn't really need washing at all: just a wipe before putting it away.

Moving swiftly on to a light lunch, we can add oats to soup for thickness and body. I prefer them just stirred in at the end so that they keep their texture, but stirred in early they'll blend in and thicken. Add enough to a small quantity of soup and we can turn it into fork food. Add a few chopped salad tomatoes, cooked meat, anything handy, and the soup has effectively become a sauce base for a main meal.

Oats work really well with fish. Herring and oatmeal is a classic combination: the oats balance and absorb the fish oils. Smoked mackerel is my favourite fish, full of flavour and goodness. Its only drawback is that it can be a bit oily; one simple solution is to mash it up with some oat-flakes into a pate. This bulks and balances it into a proper meal, which can be eaten on its own or with salad, either separately or mixed in. Simple fork food, use the same fork to prepare and to eat.

Taramasalata is another delicious fish dish that's awkward to eat. Designed for dipping, it is concentrated and falls off the fork too easily. Adding oatmeal or flakes bulks this up so that it's better balanced and more manageable. And because there's no cooking involved, the oats retain their original texture. There are hundreds of dips we can buy at the supermarket these days, all designed to be eaten with bread or vegetable dippers to add bulk and goodness. Oats serve this purpose just as well and can be stirred into any dips for delicious fork food. Add oats to your favourite coleslaw! It's cheap, easy and healthy.

Try oats in salad to lift the dressing and stop it being wasted at the bottom of the bowl. Oat-flakes and ice-cream for dessert: simply delicious.

Did we miss out on our mid-morning fly-cuppie? Flapjacks are the perfect accompaniment, but for years I wondered how to make an oat-based biscuit without adding all that fat. The great thing about oats in cooking is that they don't easily form lumps; this gives us a problem when making biscuits: they fall apart too easily. A little mechanical sidetrack here should give us some clues.

Flour goes lumpy because the individual flour particles are so small that they can't overcome the liquid surface tension and other forces pulling them together; so the flour particles cling together in lumps. With oats, the particles are much larger and can easily be knocked apart by the moving liquid. So how do we lock these mobile particles together? One way is to combine them with other lumps of different sizes. Materials with same-sized particles pour easily: think of sugar, rice, sand, gravel. This is because the particles have gaps between them and can roll over each other; as they're all much the same size, they all roll together at much the same speed. But if we fill the gaps, preferably with a sticky material, the individual particles get locked in, they can't roll and they don't pour. Think of the stones bound together by clay in your garden soil.

By mixing oatmeal with oat-flakes, we've gone some way to getting the different particle sizes. The flakes might lie in layers and slip across each other, we need them to lie in different directions so that they block each other's slip planes (which fortunately they tend to do anyway). This is how flapjacks work, with the fat and sugar acting as glue. But if we want to lose the fat and sugar, where's the glue?

The answer lies in the oat-flakes themselves: when moist they become very sticky (remember washing up after porridge?). Can we use this as a basis for a biscuit? If we're not careful we'll end up with a gluey mass. So this is where we can play with the different oat textures, with oatmeal giving us crunch and oat-flakes binding them together. We'll probably want some extra flavour: how about orange juice and sultanas? So try this at home:

Put a handful of sultanas in a micro-waveable bowl with enough orange juice to cover them, and microwave them for a couple of minutes so that the sultanas fatten with juice. Add oatmeal and oat-flakes (more meal than flakes, say twice as much) and mix them in to soak up all the juice. Because the juice is hot, the oat-flakes should already be getting sticky, but the oatmeal should remain quite gritty. Add more oats or juice as you think fit for a sticky mixture. Press this out with the back of the mixing spoon onto a greased baking tray (preferably one with little holes in it) in as thin a layer as will hold together, and bake it in a hot oven until it's done (about 10mins, or when it starts to go dark round the edges). Take it out and leave it to cool, then slide it off the tray........it's a big biscuit! Which we can then cut up into biscuit-sized bits.

We can add other flavours: apple juice for sweetness, honey for extra binding, other fruits, spices, alter the quantities as we like, cut it into different shapes. Do it as a spur-of-the-moment thing: there's so little preparation, we can make it when we've got the oven on for something else as it'll keep till later.

[I know I said you shouldn't have baking trays, but if you like biscuits you've probably got one anyway! And I admit that it is possible to make more delicious biscuits than this, but I don't believe any are as healthy while tasting as good.]

After which excitement, we're probably looking forward to our evening meal. If we're doing straight *Jette Cuisine*, we'll have our vegetables and protein all organised and cooking away. The principal role for oats is as a carbohydrate substitute: perhaps we've got enough food in the vegetables to bother about adding potatoes or pasta, or we didn't have time to cook them in the first place. Maybe we just want a little something to round off the edges of the taste. This is where we throw in some oats at the end to mix through and absorb all the juices in the pan (saves washing up again!). Oatmeal does this with a bit more crunch, whereas oat-flakes are the ultimate moppers-up.

We can use oats to make quasi-burgers: put some pieces of cheese in with some oat-flakes and other flavourings like mustard, then put the lot in the microwave for a moment to melt the cheese. When we've mixed this afterwards, the cheese and oats bind each other together and they can be pressed into burgers, balls or whatever shape we fancy. I suppose they could be heated up or fried from here on, but they don't need any further cooking than this, we can serve them there & then. We can add chopped tomatoes or olives into the mix, anything to give them flavour, as long as we've got something like cheese to bind the oats. Experiment with the tastes and textures, they're so easy and can be made in small quantities; one good way is to roll a sample into small balls and serve them as a garnish. We'll soon find out whether they're going to succeed.

As a student, I used to make meal-in-one omelettes, with various meat and vegetables cooked in a frying pan and then bound together with a couple of eggs. I would bulk these up with oat-flakes, and very successful they were. Just remember that eggs and oat-flakes are both binders, so we can end up with something very solid indeed!

Oats are wonderful disaster-fixers, quickly absorbing excess liquid or smoothing out the taste. Add with caution: a little goes a long way.

Learn from muesli: there's no reason why we can't make an evening meal along the same lines but using savoury ingredients instead. Served cold (like muesli), we could mix in chopped cooked meats, salad ingredients, nuts, and add tomato soup to give it moisture. We could do the same thing with ingredients that need cooking and serve hot: we've rediscovered porridge! But not as we've ever known it. We can turn a fruit salad into a pudding, adding bulk and losing some of the sharpness: it's better than cream!

Last thing at night, try a teaspoon of honey mixed with oats; stir until the oats wipe all the honey off the inside of the mixing cup. Just the thing to settle the stomach and aid digestion.

At this stage we're probably beginning to wonder whether we can cook anything without oats, in which case this Chapter has done its job. Of course the answer is Yes. Notice that all the above ideas involve serving oats with other ingredients, so we're certainly not going to be eating oats by themselves (even if that's what Scottish farm workers used to live off exclusively, and very well they were too).

That's why I abandoned porridge, so as to discover the range of meals we can make with this fantastically versatile, healthy and cheap ingredient.

DISASTERS
Triumph And Disaster Just The Same

As long as cooks are human there will be disasters. They come in two categories: preventable and curable. (A third type is called "terminal", concerns chip pans and fire engines, and is beyond the scope of this book.)

Prevention
So many "disasters" are not disasters at all, but just failure to come up to expectations. These are all avoidable, just by not raising expectations in the first place.

A meal cooked from a recipe is very unlikely to look as good as the picture in the book, for reasons we've already gone through in Chapter 1. It's only a disaster if it relies on appearance rather than taste, and looking good is always a poor reason for cooking a meal. If it tastes OK and just doesn't match the photo, the disaster exists only in the mind of the Cook (and of anyone who's seen the photo). If we're preparing fish and chips and it ends up looking like lasagne, for goodness sake don't call it "fish & chips". In fact, don't call it anything, we're not running a restaurant or offering a choice, so why does it need a name? It's not going to hang around long enough for its christening, it won't run away so we don't have to call it back, and if it's worth eating there are very few names which will do it justice anyway.

Following recipes (almost all of which have names) are ways of raising expectations in anyone who sees the picture or hears the name, so DON'T USE RECIPES, I know I've said it before but it's still true. And all those avoidable disasters will be avoided.

If you want to serve a soufflé, the very word encourages people to put away their taste-buds and take out their tape measures instead. Technically very interesting but precious little to do with food. If we call it an omelette instead, we get the response "how on earth do you get your omelette so light and fluffy, it's quite the lightest I've ever tasted, do give me your method so that I can try it out on my friends blah blah". I grant you this isn't electrifying entertainment, but it's better than the faint praise that doesn't quite conceal underlying contempt.

Apart from their false expectations, recipes give no help when things go differently. It's very unlikely that your cooker will be exactly the same as the recipe writer's, that you will prepare your ingredients the same way, that they will taste exactly the same, all of which affects the result. The recipe gives no guidance as to how to correct things that go wrong, because the recipe writer lives in cloud-cuckoo land (should that be cookoo?) where nothing goes wrong and the freshest ingredients are all available in exactly the right quantity just when we want them. If we can only follow a recipe, we won't know how to correct as we go. If, on the other hand, we make it up as we go along, we will correct things automatically to our own taste, because there's nothing to tell us otherwise.

One thing to be aware of: as a cook you'll think your meal should taste better than it does. This is because you know all the ingredients that have gone in, and somehow the final combination rarely lives up to all the tastes you put in. But your guests don't know this, all the little nuances you've lovingly put in. So don't tell them it's not up to your expectations, they'll only be disappointed, and then so will you. It's an anticlimax rather than a disaster, and it's avoidable just by not thinking the worst of your own creations. Self-deprecation can sometimes be charming, but this isn't one of those occasions.

And I said "rarely" rather than "never": there are the magic occasions when we think "I thought it was going to be good, but I didn't dare think THIS good!" Yes it happens, if we give ourselves the freedom to allow it to happen.

The rules of prevention must therefore include:
- Don't give food names. By all means say what's in it, in case of allergies, but let the food speak for itself.

- If the food doesn't have a name then we're not using a recipe (because they all have names), and we avoid all those problems as well.
- Don't imagine things are worse than they are, by imagining they're going to be better and then being disappointed by the reality.

These disasters are fundamentally all to do with image and expectation, and are the most trivial. More important are those that concern taste. And these are caused by over-cooking. Why? Because the alternative is to under-cook, in which case we cook a little longer until it's properly done.

Cure

I had an example of cure last night: I was cooking with an unfamiliar ingredient, in this case butter beans. The Better Half decided on a whim that she'd like butter beans, and the only ones we had in were dried. I forget how much these expand when they're soaked and cooked, so when I'd added my other veg (onion, broad beans, green beans, cherry tomatoes & red pepper) I still had butter beans with some additives. At least I knew I wouldn't need potatoes! I added the sliced smoked sausage at the end, which I knew would add Salt and succulence, but the mix still tasted Smooth, slightly Sour and was a bit too dry; in other words rather dull and not particularly nice. It needed a little acidity but with subtlety, and liquid without being drowned. So I added a squirt of red wine to give Sharp with a little Sweet, and a couple of spoons of yoghurt to give a bit of Smooth and Sharp. The dish was transformed from "this is inedible" to "let's have this one again".

Once we go down this route to fix a disaster, the result is always in doubt (which is part of the excitement), but we've moved the goalposts to span between "nice" and "fantastic". In the above case I was lucky and I got the best possible result ("tucked away in the right-hand corner"), but even when it goes the other way we've still got an enjoyable meal and live for another day. And all I did was to look at the Taste & Texture I'd got, and then decide what to add to push them in the right direction, using what I had to hand.

It's not rocket science, and come to think of it a dose of tomato ketchup would probably have achieved much the same effect (if not quite so subtle). But fixing disasters is just as personal as selecting ingredients in the first place: it's getting to the Taste & Texture we want, with what we have to hand. Indeed it's almost the same as making a new recipe, but most of the ingredients have already been supplied. So from that point of view it's easier than starting from scratch.

The only problem is that we're doing it on the hop. If we need time to think, just take the pan off the heat: the last thing we need to do is burn the food as well. It'll cook a bit more before it cools down, but there are very few things that will be ruined by so doing. (Eggs are probably the most intolerant of such a delay, unless they're hard-boiled, then they're fine.) When we've worked out what to add, we're back up and running. It's best to add a little of our corrective measure at a time and taste it, just to confirm we're heading in the direction we want; then we just continue until we've got a result.

Another way to deal with disaster is dilution: if our meal is too salty, we could double the quantities of the other ingredients. But do we want twice as much? Probably not (we'd have made twice as much in the first place), so cure is better.

Here are a few shortcut cures to get us started, based on our preparing a main course and needing to add a quick-fix at the end.

Too:	Add:	And a little:
Sweet	**Sour** (herbs), **Sharp** (wine, lemon juice).	Salt, Spicy.
Sour	**Sweet** (apple juice, peas).	Salt, Sharp.
Sharp	**Smooth** (bread, oats, mushrooms, whisky).	Sour, Salt.
Smooth	**Sharp** (wine, orange juice).	Salt, Spicy.
Salt	**Smooth** (bread, oats, mushrooms).	Sour, Sweet.
Spicy	**Smooth** (bread, oats, mushrooms, yoghurt).	Sharp, Sweet.

Remember these are only first ideas; adapt them and develop fixes of your own. At this stage, adding Sour normally means herbs, which pack all sorts of other beneficial side effects. Try to get combined effects using one additive: for example, baby tomatoes and orange juice both give Sharp and Sweet.

And what about Burnt? Yes, we can all occasionally overcook, perhaps we got a 'phone call when the meal was almost ready. Can't start again, so we need a fix. Burnt is essentially Sour with a bit of Smooth. Cure it with Sweet and Sharp, and a bit of Salt. Add orange juice (little by little and taste), which lifts and neutralises the carbon off the bottom of the pan, then finally salt to taste. And why not complete it with a little Spicy black pepper?

So this is the other reason why I went rather laboriously into Taste & Texture. Once we've understood the Six Savours, we can use them to prepare a new dish beforehand (Build A Meal), and to adjust a new meal on the hop (Disaster-Fixing). We've deliberately removed the constraint of aiming for a particular target (a well-known dish) and we can move the goalposts in any direction we want to arrive at something new and special.

No Trouble!

BUILDING A MEAL
The Daily Impress

Throughout this book I've tried to build in as much personal freedom as possible, giving you, Dear Reader, the choice as to what you'll eat and how. But a clean sheet of paper is not without disadvantage: where to begin? With a recipe book we can flip through until something takes our fancy, but how eye-catching is a blank page?

To start with, we need a bit of thinking time, and as this is something we'll do almost every day, we need to fit it into our own routine. The best time is before we start to prepare (not afterwards, ha ha) but not so long beforehand that we miss the mood of the moment. For me, the main meal of the day is in the evening, so the perfect time to start thinking about it is on the way home.

And this is how it works.

Start with various mood questions like "How hungry am I?" "Do we want something heavy or light?" "Is it summer or winter?" Do we want hot or cold?" "How much time have I got?" "How many courses?" (This is easy: the answer's "One!" 99 times out of 100.) "How many will we be?" "What will they want?" (This one's only hard if you let it: most people will eat what's put in front of them as long as they're hungry and it's not burnt.)

We don't have to ask or answer all these questions, or any others I've missed, but in going through the process we'll quickly get a picture as to whether it's likely to be pasta for six or salad for one. Which is enough to get us to the next stage.

"What did we have yesterday?" We won't be wanting the same thing today, so this is a big steer. We might also be able to answer "what are we having tomorrow" as well, for example Friday night is always pizza. If we had pasta yesterday, it can be anything else today, so that leaves potatoes, rice, bread, oats, just lots of veg, plenty of choice. If yesterday's sauce was tomato-based, why not a white cheese sauce today? Or curry, or chilli. Or we could leave out the sauce altogether and prepare something drier, perhaps flavoured with garlic and herbs; this might point us towards cubes of toast instead of potatoes to emphasise the crunch; or dry-roast potatoes. If the food's drier, we'll want to drink more: is this OK? If not, perhaps we should stick with sauce. If meat yesterday, why not fish today? Perhaps a tin of tuna. You get the point.

This is not to say we should change every single ingredient from what we had yesterday, that would be crazy: "I had onions yesterday, so I shan't touch another until tomorrow!" Indeed we may have enjoyed yesterday's meal so much that we'll say "Let's have the same again!" The only danger in this is that duplicate meals make a balanced diet less likely in the long run. And the same meal never tastes quite as good on the second day. So ring the changes each day, whether they're minor or a complete revamp.

This is not to say we should plan an entire week's eating in advance: how can we when we don't know how we'll feel at the time, what the weather's going to be like, who's going to be in, and so on. We only need to remember what we ate yesterday, and preferably have some inkling of what we might eat tomorrow, and that's enough. By this reasoning, we could repeat our meals every three days if we wanted. But I don't think we would.

This is all background, now we can get to the substance: "What have we got in the house?" And perhaps even more important: "What do we need to eat up?" I know this second point harks back to a wartime mentality of 'waste not want not', and that there are folk who like to show that they have money to throw away. But for those of us with better things to do with our spare cash, let's make some attempt to use ingredients that would have to be thrown out if left a couple of days longer.

And let's not hanker after any ingredients we haven't got in at the time (unless we're planning a shopping trip on the way home). Make a note of it for next time we go to the supermarket, and then get on with what we've got. "Necessity is the Mother of Invention", and as often as not we'll come up with something better than our first thought.

So we start with the perishables and look in the fridge, on the vegetable rack and in the bread bin. (If we cooked yesterday, we'll remember what's left so we don't have to wait until we get home.) Then we can check out the dry cupboards and tins.

We might be a bit disappointed that our first ingredients are things we need to get rid of. In fact it's no bad thing to be led in a certain direction, to start filling in our blank sheet of paper. Once started, the pattern is much easier to continue and complete.

Of course we can start with brand-new ingredients, because we've got nothing that's not fresh (oh happy day). Now we have a choice to make, unless we already have a specific meal in mind (sounds like a recipe to me); or there's only one thing left (which makes the choice for us). Choice is tough; nice-to-have but tough. So when we're feeling tired at the end of a hard day, there's something to be said for letting the things that need to be eaten up make this choice for us.

Environmentally friendly too!

The questions we ask ourselves split the Meal-Building process into Mood and Food. One is all about ambience, effect, context; the other with the building blocks we have available. We play off one against the other as we go until we reach our target.

But this is all terribly abstract, so I'll bare my soul (only by way of example you understand) and go through the thought process of evening meals for a few successive days. I'm not making any puddings: there'll be plenty of food in the main dish, and if anyone wants anything else there's fruit salad in the fridge, ice cream in the freezer, biscuits in the barrel. And it's not the height of summer, so we can't get away with just salads.

Monday is easy: I'm assuming we had Sunday Lunch, roast meat and veg, and there are leftovers to be dealt with. So the first decision of the basic ingredients is already made, and it's just a question of how we spark them up. I generally start off by softening an onion before adding the cooked vegetables; will that be enough? If not, we can sub out the onion with carrots or green beans. White sauce or red? We can use tomatoes for red but I think we might have them with pasta tomorrow, so we'll use a little red wine instead. A few herbs? Mustard? Or we could curry it instead. Perhaps bit of garlic near the end of cooking (it's stronger this way). Cut the meat into small pieces and add at the end: it only needs warming as it's already cooked, so don't boil it to blazes and make it tough. Check the quantity, taste, and serve.

Tuesday I've got plenty of carrots, onions, pasta, a tin of tomatoes and cheese, so tomato pasta is easy. Add some dried herbs while the pasta is cooking. The carrots will sweeten the tomatoes. A squirt of red wine towards the end will give the taste more body. It's all a bit red: let's have a few green beans or some broccoli. Or peas for sweetness if we don't have any carrots. A few mushrooms? Some cooked sausage or salami? Let's add the sausage early so that its flavour leaches into the sauce. Check the quantity and taste: is it a little sour? We can add a dash of jam or apple juice. More salt? A few chopped olives. We can slice some cheese into strips to sprinkle over as well. A little more zest? Some grainy mustard or a few chopped capers. OK now? Serve.

Wednesday I'm looking for a bit of a change after two sloppy meals, and I've got some cabbage and cooked meats that need eating, these work well together. So we chop the cabbage, ham, garlic sausage, salami into strips and zhet them up together; we're aiming for crisp so we don't want to add liquid. How's the quantity looking (we're going to add some bread as well)? Some green beans, baby corn or mushrooms will do (careful of the liquid in the mushrooms), or a handful of peas from the freezer. Meantime let's toast a couple of slices of bread (say 1 slice/person) and chop them into little squares. Chop a few little tomatoes and add them to the pot for sharpness, stir in, and then add the toast pieces last thing and stir to soak up any remaining juice. Check quantity, taste, texture. Does it look a bit dry at the last moment? Add a blob of yoghurt, with a sprig of parsley if we want it pretty, and serve.

Thursday the whole family is eating together, so I'm going for quantity and less exotic tastes. We've had pasta and toast on the previous two days, so let's use potatoes today. I'm right out of meat, but I've got plenty of cheese and some tins of tuna. Some onions and one last carrot. I could use hard-boiled eggs if it was for the children only, but these are out courtesy of Senior Management. Some milk. I could do plain cheese & potato pie, but I'm starting to think in terms of pizza tomorrow, so I'll probably use the tuna and maybe just sub it out with some cheese. So we'll slice and zhet plenty of potatoes to start with, in our largest non-stick pan, while we chop onions and the carrot. No salt: we'll use the brine from the tuna. Add the onions and carrot, and let them sweat a little before we add a bit of milk: not so much the potatoes are swimming, but enough to make a bit of sauce which will thicken as the potatoes break down. And some frozen peas. Mushrooms? Cut a little cheese into strips. When the peas have thawed and are stirred in, we can fork the tuna from the tin (so that it spreads through easily) and add its brine. Check quantity and taste: do we need more spark? Green olives are excellent with tuna, and a few cherry tomatoes for zest and colour. Stir in the cheese until it's melted to thicken the sauce and serve.

Friday, and I was thinking about pizza but I've only got in the freezer, and I've plenty of sliced bread that needs eating up, and cheese too. So "pizza" and salad it will be; fine for the children as well, they can eat theirs at the first sitting, we'll have ours later. They can make their own salad (which will be lettuce, cucumber, tomatoes, chopped pickled onions and green olives, salad cream and vinegar if I'm any judge) and we'll make ours including more exotic leaves, avocados and fresh basil. The pizza is effectively cheese-on-toast aimed at the pizza market. We take a rectangular baking tray and put on slices of bread tight up against each other. (Not a bad idea to have rubbed a bit of oil over the tray if we think the cheese is going to spill, which it surely will) We should get four or six slices on at a time, depending on the size of the tray. This is obvious if we've got square bread, but if it's rounded at the top then leave the rounds to the outside of the group. A nice touch, if we have a thick-slice toaster, is to toast two slices in one slot back-to-back beforehand: then the toasted side goes down on the baking tray and the soft side gets the topping. Or we can pre-toast one side under the grill, which should be on by now (unless we're oven-baking the pizza). Or we can just use soft bread. Spread tomato puree thinly on each slice (or the children might prefer ketchup), then cover with sliced cheese (not so messy as grated). We can use different sorts of cheese (eg cheddar, orange mild and white mature, a bit of blue) and arrange them in a pattern. We can add anything else we want under the cheese: herbs, slices of onion or mushroom, garlic, chillies(!), whatever we've seen (or would like to see) at the pizza house. Then put under the grill and serve when the cheese is bubbling. Unless we want deep-pan pizza: in which case we slap another layer of bread on top of the bubbling cheese with another layer of toppings (the same as before or different, how about grainy mustard instead of tomato puree this time?) Put under the grill again and serve when the top cheese is bubbling. Unless we went round again, but how much bread do we want to use up, and how much headroom have we got under the grill? So perhaps we'll leave it at two layers.

Saturday we're going to the butcher to get the joint for Sunday lunch (preferably different from the previous two weeks), so we can look out something special for Saturday night, or we might have fish, or carry-out, or...........and then we're into the loop for next week.

The main excuse for not cooking this way is "I haven't got the imagination", but we can see from the above that there is actually very little imagination involved. What it takes is an understanding of where we want to get to, what we've got to get there, and letting ourselves go with the flow. We only have to avoid creating imaginary obstacles, in which case lack of imagination is probably helpful. We end up with practicality and novelty, which are in turn the Father and Child of Invention.

Quite apart from which, we've discovered a rhyming equation:
Mood + Food = Good

MISCELLANY
Not Quite JR's Ma

Now for a few little articles which don't merit an entire chapter themselves, but are still worth a mention.

Barbecues

Barbecues are good food ruined. I know the idea of huddling round an open fire has its attraction on a typical British summer's day, but it's not necessary to cook good food on it as well. If the food were leftovers, there might be some excuse, but we've bought quality burgers, sausages, chicken, steak, which are all delicious when treated with a little care.

It's not that they can't be cooked on a barbecue, but it's a bit like the one-legged channel swimmer: the determination is admirable, but it's still better for most of us to use the Tunnel. Feasibility doesn't equal desirability. It's hard enough to cook sausages and burgers in a conventional frying pan indoors, burning the underside while the top cools. But compared with the feeble heat of sullen embers below and a strong arctic breeze above blowing smoke in our eyes, the frypan approach is simplicity itself. To guard against the meat being left raw, we barbecue until it's burnt beyond recognition, and we still manage to serve it cold. Garnished with ash. We spend so long waiting for the food to cook, drinking ourselves silly, that we end up being prepared to eat anything, including that suspiciously red and chewy bit of chicken leg that we know is raw.

In short, there's nothing we barbecue that wouldn't be better cooked indoors. If we're interested in the food's taste and yet want to eat it outdoors, we should cook it indoors and then bring it out. All the party-goers can eat outside, which is what they came for, without being smothered in smoke, and the food will be better. The cook(s) will be away from the party (as before), but for less time and out of the smoke, with results which are better appreciated.

Given all this, why do people have barbecues, when there are easier ways of partying outdoors? I think it's the hardship element: it's a Male Thing, saying to the little woman indoors "You take a break from the cooking my dear, I'll wrestle with the elements and knock up something mediocre against all odds while you take a back seat, this is Man's Work" and so on. We get out all the paraphernalia, gauntlets, loud aprons, hats and tongs, so as to show how we can turn good meat into charcoal.

Gents, why not do cooking in the kitchen instead? It was never an exclusively female preserve, and you'll find more pleasure in cooking food the way you like, rather than just fighting the elements. It's better than leaving the choice of your meal to someone who's hooked on chocolate. (And Ladies, if you think the comment unfair, when did you last buy your man a box of chocolates?)

Gas Mark I

Jette Cuisine is easiest cooked on gas. It's quick and instinctive: sometimes we need to turn the heat down as things start to catch, or up as we need to hurry things along. Either way, it's easier if the heat responds instantly. It's possible to cook this way on electric (particularly on a halogen hob) as I've done in various holiday cottages (take your own non-stick pan!), but this involves moving pans half-on and -off hot-plates to achieve the same effect, so go for gas every time if you have the choice.

To keep the balance, use an electric oven, which is cleaner than gas and gives us back-up in the event that either fuel supply gets cut off. And we're not tempted to pop our heads in when things don't turn out as well as we'd like.

Gas Mark II

The more sensitive among you may care to skip this section; realists read on.

I remember reading an article on gas in an In-Flight magazine on the way to America. The woman being interviewed was claiming that certain food gave her gas, and I was struggling to come to terms with petrol discounting, I knew fuel was cheap in the States, but I thought this an unusual promotion, until I realised she was talking about farting.

Funny how little is written about this subject. Well perhaps not: I suppose there isn't enough to fill an entire book, but this doesn't mean there is nothing constructive to say either. It shouldn't just be reduced to schoolboy sniggers and embarrassed censorship. After all, we all do it. We've all wandered through the perfume counters at a department store (they're always on the way out aren't they) with a heightened sense of smell, when we notice something unusual in the air. We know it wasn't us (we do, don't we), and looking around the otherwise deserted counters, are forced to the inescapable conclusion that the lady with the immaculate make-up, dripping with jewellery, has just dropped one. She, of course, hadn't seen us and so took the opportunity to discreetly let one out.

We've all been there Madam! Although not everyone advertises it to the extent of one trombone player I knew who set light to his on the Central Line of the London Underground (before they made all the carriages non-smoking). Perhaps we should have farting rooms at the office, the same way as we have smoking rooms, though not of course the same place: that could be extremely dangerous. What would it be called? On balance the best thing is probably to go for a quick stroll outside.

The point is, it does us good! The unfashionable truth is that farty food is healthy food (I'm afraid 14pints of lager doesn't qualify). It just isn't quite so good for those in our immediate vicinity, although if they're getting their share as well, everyone benefits overall. Gas working through the digestive system massages it on its way and prevents things stagnating. Particularly if the gas comes from eating vegetables, which are doing us good in their own right; even the gas from fizzy drinks is some help. I don't have any medical evidence for this or results of a detailed study, it's just common sense. Every part of our body benefits from exercise, of which massage is a gentle form. We can massage our digestive system externally by deep breathing, with our diaphragm pushing it up and down. Gas transfer supplies an internal massage. Equally, if we let the gas build up, as well as getting stomach pains, we end up with the dreaded Floater, that object of so much futile toilet-brush sword-play: "Get down you brute!" So adopt the controlled release strategy, as considerately to those about you as you can.

Above all, don't let it dominate your life as that American lady did, who set her diet by whether or not it gave her wind. She was nicely dressed, but I've never seen anyone photograph so miserable. And I can't say I'm surprised.

Germ Warfare
This one's a bit controversial as well, but we're on a roll with the alternative views at the moment, so here goes.

Isn't it ironic that we're now plagued by "superbugs", many of them associated with our food, when we've managed to get rid of diseases like smallpox, and more is known (and practised) about food hygiene than was ever done in the past? I know that the superbugs are largely blamed on pill-popping in the Far East, where antibiotics are freely available in the corner shop, but their effect is maximised by our own lack of immune system.

Personally I don't believe in superbugs. I do believe in infections that evolve to outsmart antibiotics, but this isn't desperately difficult as antibiotics are a crude and blundering instrument, wiping out the good bacteria in one's body as well as the bad. Any self-respecting bug will get round antibiotics in time, without aspiring to the title of "super".

What's this got to do with food? It's too pure. It's too clean to exercise our immune system, which like any other part of our body needs to be worked just to keep it in good order, let alone build it up. This is nothing new: it's the principle of homeopathy, and it's also common sense; without our immune system, the human race would have died out centuries before the invention of antibiotics. The result is that our immune system becomes weak from pure food, then when something nasty comes along – probably a ready-cooked meal from the chill counter that hasn't been properly heated through – we have nothing to fight it with, and keel over.

What to do? Avoid hyper-hygiene. This is not to say that we should go in search of filth, but that a certain low level of dirt is actually beneficial in exercising the immune system and increasing our resistance to trivial infections. What my parents used to call "good clean dirt". I remember the time I dropped the scalding dish of family supper: we ate macaroni cheese off the floor (not literally you understand, but this featured in its preparation), and our main concern was for fragments of glass rather than germs. It was either that or go hungry. I've no doubt this attitude has been instrumental in my rude good health ever since.

Not what manufacturers of disinfectant might like us to hear, but true nonetheless. We should vary our healthy diet with a bit of junk food, and not treat Use-By dates as Holy Writ. Don't avoid the slightly mouldy grape: it's only penicillin after all. Peeling fruit and veg may get rid of traces of fertiliser or pesticide, but it also deprives us of the goodness within the peel (much of which is close to the skin) and the boost our immune system gets from processing such chemicals. So if you're one of those people who think "Urh!-Urh!-Germs!-Urh!", think again.

Of course there are conflicting arguments here, and none of us (not even the self-styled experts) knows whether it's better to eat a little chemical with a lot of goodness, or to cut both out altogether. But the world is a dangerous place and we cannot avoid infection forever;

this suggests to me that it is better to feed the body and immune system than to feed neither.

It's an attitude of mind: do we seriously think that a silly little bug is going to bring down a great and marvellous machine like the human body? It may exercise the immune system for a while, we may have to go for a lie-down, but dealing with little things that do us harm makes us stronger in the long run.

Health & Safety
While we're on doom-&-gloom, don't forget that we're working in a room with naked flames, flammable materials and offensive weapons. Not something to dwell on, but make sure we know how to react to something catching fire, and have some plasters handy in the kitchen. And check them periodically lest your children play them away.

Roasts
I wasn't originally planning on writing anything about roasts; after all, they're not exactly *Jette Cuisine*. But family proof-readers suggested I should put in something about Sunday Lunch, so here it is. At least the "Don't Throw Anything Away" principle applies.

Roast potatoes start off by being split in half by length, breadth and depth (we'll end up with eight pieces from each potato). The smallest will cook fastest, and we can serve "Three Different Types of Potato" (overdone, underdone and just right). Or split the largest potatoes that way and cut the smaller ones into similar sized pieces for a more uniform effect. No peeling! Then they're boiled in a little water, with the lid on: cover them with water at most, better only to half-cover them. I know I said "Never Boil Anything", but this is going to end up as gravy so it's OK. And I've tried zhetting potatoes before roasting, but they don't open up quite so well: they need to absorb water to become softer, so a par-boil is better. Meantime heat up the oven to about 150°C. When the potatoes start to look slightly floury (about 10mins), don't drain them: spoon them into a roasting tray with a few drops of olive oil in the bottom. Don't worry if some of the water comes over as well, because the next task is to arrange the potatoes with a flat side on the oily bottom of the tray, and then spread the oil & water over the potatoes. The water will boil off in the oven, and it's astonishing how little oil is needed to brown the potatoes. Let them roast in the oven this way up until they're nearly done, then turn them a few times towards the finish. They should take a bit over an hour this way, depending how hot the oven and how crunchy we like them.

Meat starts off completely wrapped up in foil, unless it's pork with crackling (which needs a very high heat early on) where we cover the exposed meat only, not the skin. I chop up garlic and herbs, mustard or horse-radish sauce, and mix them on the chopping board before placing them in a little bed of flavours on the foil for the meat to lie on. Just before finally wrapping up the meat, I give it a little squirt of red wine for moisture and flavour. So the first part of the roasting in foil keeps juices and flavours in, and represents most of the cooking (unless it's to be underdone beef). We take meat out of the foil and give it a final open roast with the potatoes (to crisp up the outside) some 15mins before serving. The remaining herbs and juices from the foil go into the vegetable water (which was the potato water).

Vegetables can be cooked either in the potato water (which transfers some of their taste to the gravy), or roasted with the potatoes (carrots, parsnips and peppers are excellent for this). Do both: roast the thick ends of the carrots and boil (or steam: there's not much water left) the rest. Better still, zhet the vegetables and use the potato water for gravy. Roll the roasting veg in a little olive oil on a serving plate, then roast in the oven for about 45mins. The steamed (or zhetted) vegetables start long after this: carrots, cabbage, broccoli stalks can be brought to boil well after the meat has been removed from its foil: 10mins is enough. Add broccoli florets and frozen peas at the end as they only need a minute or so.

Gravy is nature's way of cleaning the roasting tray of all the wonderful burnt-on flavours, so we don't struggle to wash them up. When the meat and potatoes are cooked, remove them from the roasting tray onto serving plates, and add a bit of flour and a squirt of red wine or sherry to whatever's left in the roasting tray, <u>off the heat</u>. We can cold-mix the flour in with the wine to get rid of any lumps, then add some potato water, stir and bring to the boil. As the gravy boils, using a fish-slice to stir, we can feel all the little bits of potato and so on come unstuck from the roasting tray. Then turn off the heat, for now.

Serving is the part requiring most co-ordination, particularly if you want to carve at table. I'm a messy carver, so I do this in the kitchen, making sure that anyone who wants to see the meat in its piece gets the chance beforehand. (Put plates in the oven to warm now.) This gets round the problem of the meat "resting" (which allows it to tenderise – and become very cold – after the stress of cooking). The meat can be sliced before resting (it rests much quicker in slices) and then put back in a warm oven. It cooks some more back in the oven, so leave it underdone to allow for this, and it releases more juices for the gravy during resting. Drain any final vegetable water into the gravy, and dish up the potatoes and veg onto warm plates. Switch on the heat under the gravy, pour in the meat juices, serve the meat and then the gravy. Done!

Salmon

Wonderful stuff, salmon. Delicious, healthy and (since the advent of fish-farming) fabulously cheap. Much to the delight of restaurateurs who invariably put it on the menu with comments such as "Lovingly Prepared Using The Choicest Ingredients". (What does "choicest" actually mean anyway? Most chosen? By whom? Not surprising if it's the restaurateurs because they actually mean "cheapest".) Only one problem: it stinks when it's cooked.

Not every way it's cooked, mind you; just almost every way. And certainly when it's pan-fried, which is how it's done on TV because it goes such a nice colour, and the way restaurants do it for the same reason. Unless we have an extractor fan the size of a jumbo jet (which is unlikely to win us the lasting gratitude of our next-door neighbours), our rooms will smell for hours if not days, and we'll be left with a frying pan which is good for nothing else.

It gets to the food it's cooked with: salmon is one of the few ingredients that doesn't enhance its companions in the pot. That's why this little section has been relegated to "Miscellany" and is excluded from the main body of *Jette Cuisine*.

So here is a method which gets round the smell, and in the process produces the most delicious tasting fish. As with all the great discoveries, it was accidental and is brilliantly simple. It was made by The Better Half when she was simplifying her diet, and goes like this: put the salmon on its own in a piece of aluminium foil, wrap it up, and bake it in the oven until it starts to smell nicely of salmon (or about 20mins/lb @ 150°C if you want to mix your units). Then take it out and serve. That's it: no oil, no salt, no herbs, no wine, no garlic, nothing. There's enough oil and water in the fish to steam without it sticking, the fish just lifts off any skin which stays in the foil.

Doesn't sound much does it? Tasting is believing.

Shopping
We're sometimes told that there's no such thing as seasonal food anymore: we can get anything we want all year round (apart from obviously festive things like Christmas Puddings). Even mince pies and Easter Eggs appear pretty much year-round.

But at a more subtle level, we still have seasons; indeed we have two lots of seasons. We may be able to get strawberries year-round, but they'll be much more plentiful - and cheaper – in summer. This applies to all fruits and most veg, and is largely understood and predictable. The other season occurs entirely at the whim of the supermarket or food manufacturer, and is the special offer or promotion. Though less predictable, it is just as good a season for buying particular goods. From a *Jette Cuisine* standpoint, the special offer is particularly valuable as it injects variety and surprise into our daily diet.

Shopping for *Jette Cuisine* differs from normal shopping because, without recipes, we have much less need of a list. We can be more instinctive, more flexible, and take greater advantage of seasonal goods and promotions. This applies particularly to perishables.

Food can be divided into two main categories: perishable and non-perishable. The latter are items we should always have in as they have limitless shelf-life, and include the likes of (dry) pasta, rice, flour, oats, pulses, tins, oil, vinegar, salt, spices, dried herbs; all things we can keep in to expand other ingredients into a balanced meal. Mustard, sauces, ketchup and pickles have near limitless shelf-life as well, and onions can be kept longer than other vegetables. So we should replace any of these that we have nearly finished, regardless of whether we intend to eat them in the next week or so.

Having our shelves stocked with such non-perishables, we know we won't starve: if our tins include tomatoes and tuna, we can make ourselves some very presentable dishes without resorting to perishables at all. Then we can pick up perishables as they take our fancy: they'll need to because we'll be eating them within a week. These will consist of some regular items (such as salad ingredients and fruit) which we know will turn out useful, and some will be completely opportunistic.

By way of example, here's my subconscious shopping list; I've subdivided perishables into "staples" (not the little metal things you comedian, reminds me how our eldest, learning to ride a bike, was surprised that her yoghurt contained stabilisers) and "luxuries".

- **Non-Perishables**: pasta, rice, flour, oatflakes, oatmeal, lentils, chickpeas, butter beans, tinned tomatoes, baked beans, tuna, anchovies, tube of tomato puree, light olive oil, extra virgin olive oil, pickled onions, raisins, sultanas, boxed apple juice & orange juice, boxed red wine, dried milk, honey, jam, salt, black pepper, mustard (english & grainy), olives, ketchup, salad cream, horse radish sauce, tartare sauce, capers, pickles, chilli sauce, worcester sauce, curry powder, paprika, chilli powder, mixed dried herbs, stock cubes. We should never run out of these, they last for ages (with the possible exception of the red wine) and always come in handy sometime. Assuming you have a freezer, add frozen peas, vanilla ice cream to this list. Don't forget aluminium foil, cling-wrap, kitchen towel and washing-up liquid.

- **Staples**: bread, potatoes, butter, eggs, cheese, milk, yoghurt, smoked sausage, carrots, onions, french beans, red cabbage, broccoli, mushrooms, garlic, lettuce, cucumber, tomatoes, oranges, apples, bananas, fresh parsley and herbs.
- **Luxuries**: meat (uncooked and cooked), fish, seasonal veg fruit & salad, and make up the rest yourself!

Notice that the largest category is Non-Perishables, so we can largely disengage the brain and still survive. And no sugar on my list: there's plenty more interesting sweetness about.

The best thing about shopping this way is that we don't need to be driven by thoughts of a particular recipe, and worry that we may have forgotten a vital ingredient. Better to buy too little and sub it out with non-perishables than to throw things away. We can just wander through the aisles picking up a selection of staples and luxuries as they catch our eye (preferably because they're cheap!), confident in our ability to make meals out of them in due course. Not only does this reduce stress levels in the shopper, it helps to stimulate variety in diet which is likely to improve our health. And our cash goes further. The sort of shopping even a man can enjoy!

Soup
At last an excuse to boil something up. For best results, boil vegetables in stock rather than plain water; hence stock cubes on the shopping list. Throw in dried herbs as well. Ingredients can include

any veg that needs finishing up. Use potatoes for thickening. Boil for plenty of time to get everything soft. Any pre-cooked ingredients, leftovers, cooked meats can go in at the end. We eat more soup in winter, and any left over can be used as the basis for the next day's.

We can liquidise the soup in a blender, but this involves messy transfers of hot liquids, so using a masher to smooth out the largest lumps is easier. It also leaves more texture in the soup, which is no bad thing.

The soup doesn't have to be liquidised, the leftovers don't have to be pre-cooked. Today it was snowing and I had more mushrooms and milk than I immediately knew what to do with; and rather a glut of garlic. So mushroom soup it was, using finely chopped mushrooms, zhetted, with a hunfy of oatmeal, milk and a vegetable stock cube; and those cloves of garlic, and a couple of thin slices of mature cheddar melted in for salt. I've never tasted soup so creamy smooth, yet the milk was semi-skimmed so it was down to the oatmeal. The mushrooms more than held their own in this company, so "leftover" soup needn't taste leftover.

No leftovers? Then use a tin as the basis. Try zhetted onions, thickening (oatmeal for speed, potatoes if time), vegetable stock (cube & water) and a tin of baked beans and/or chopped tomatoes. Fabulous tomato and/or bean soup.

All the taste rules apply as before, and anything we thought worth having in the house is probably fine in our soup. It's likely to end up tasting quite vegetably, so be ready with the red wine or a tin of baked beans as necessary; then serve with grated cheese or a blob of yoghurt with some scenic parsley. These will blow the socks off conventional *borsch* or *minestrone*!

Washing Up

The Bishop of Salisbury came to supper when I was a child: he was a friend of my father's from schooldays. Of course we asked him to help with the washing up (which was considered something of a social event in our household), and he agreed to help, but he limited himself to his 39 Articles, which among five diners is a lot of gobbling rods.

In the age of the dishwasher, this gentle social activity – when people are brought together by turn rather than by choice, for a time determined only by their skill at the task – is becoming sadly lost. And how it warmed our hands in winter before central heating was common. It's still more economical and sociable than the dishwasher, and often simpler too: by the time we've rinsed in preparation for the machine, we might just as well have washed up. And as we've done our best in *Jette Cuisine* to limit our washing up, a dishwasher is less use. So here are a few tips on this dying art from one who washed up with The Best.

All skilled washers-up have their own method, but there are two main principles:
1. Use the hottest water possible, so that the grease lifts off and the crocks are virtually self-drying. This minimises the risk of the dryer-up having a tea-towel so wringing wet as to be ineffectual.
2. Keep the washing water clean (and hot) for as long as possible. Nothing so dispiriting as having a washed plate handed back with yet another rogue pea or tea-leaf stuck on, from using water like dilute minestrone.

To me, these are the only fundamental principles. My father used boiling water from the kettle (a little extreme), a soap powder called "Omo" (because washing up liquid hadn't been invented), and a bowl of rinsing water (because Omo wasn't self-rinsing). These days, we don't need the rinsing water because of advances in detergent technology, but we should still use the hottest water we can get: we just dip the dishes in rather than our hands so that we don't get scalded.

The way this works for me is to use a bowl smaller than the sink (leaving a gap down the side), filled with the hottest tap water and washing up liquid. Take a dirty plate and scoop a little water on it to rinse any food down beside the washing-up bowl into the sink, and then wash the plate clean: this saves dirtying the water in the bowl. (And of course I've got ahead of myself here: start with the cleanest items, which are generally glasses, followed by cutlery, plates, and finish with the dirty pans.) By keeping our plates and hands out of the water, we keep it hot and clean, so that it shouldn't need to be changed.

By the same token, putting a pile of plates in to soak makes the water cold and dirty all at once. (The ecologically sound way to rinse plates is with the tepid water we have to run before the tap becomes hot.) Fewer water changes mean less time taken, and clean water means fewer returns.

No doubt you will develop your own method: there's no skill that cannot be improved with practice, which turns a chore into an art. Treat your washing-up water with respect, and it will repay you handsomely.

I hope I haven't laboured the point, but not even *Jette Cuisine* can get rid of washing up completely, though it can help: which of us hasn't started to cook and found our pan is still dirty from yesterday? Don't wash it up, think whether the leftover *bolognaise* will improve what we're about to cook today: fish pie – probably not; curry – yes. (I'm not suggesting this if we've uncovered the pan after a fortnight's search, but the following day will be fine: any bacteria surviving yesterday's cooking will be wiped out during today's. So don't put in washing-up liquid to soak!) We get instant extra flavour. Far from the cheffy roasting of bones, adding a bottle of wine, straining it through muslin then reducing the lot down, this stock adds individuality and comes easier than no stock at all.

TO FINISH
Natural Sciences

This has taken me longer than I thought.

It's been something of a voyage of discovery, with quite a few back-tracks and detours along the way. Having found my way out at the other side, I can see why it was such a struggle. This was never going to be a conventional cookbook, but I had no idea quite how different it would turn out to be.

It's a bit like the difference between Physics & Chemistry: both sciences, but with completely different ways of thinking. With Chemistry, we need to learn masses of chemical formulae and equations. There are rules to help, but much of it involves learning huge amounts of data by rote. By contrast, with Physics we only need to learn about four concepts and everything can be worked out from first principles. The concepts are harder to grasp than chemical formulae, but once understood, the rest is easy.

Conventional cooking is like Chemistry: there's any number of recipes for any number of dishes. Some standard methods that repeat themselves, but if we want to arrive at the right compound on the plate, we have to put it through the correct chemical reaction. The only variable is how much we make, which leads us to double (or half) the ingredient quantities, but nothing very creative.

Jette Cuisine is like Physics: understand the basic concepts and we can go anywhere we like. My difficulty was in identifying and understanding these basic concepts, in order to put them down on paper. I've got them down to four, which are, in order of decreasing importance:

1. Taste
2. No Waste
3. Haste
4. No Paste

The best that can be said about these is that they rhyme, and so perhaps remembering the first (and most obvious) will help recall the others. Each has associated meanings that we can summarise below.

Taste
- Ultimately, it's all down to personal taste: you know what you like (or are likely to like) so cook accordingly. Not as a chef who's a stranger to you might say.
- Taste is more important than appearance: it is food after all, it's not for mounting on a wall (not the ultimate accolade, as any parent of small children knows). By all means make it look attractive as well, but not at the expense of flavour.
- We can make almost any taste we want by combining standard ingredients in our kitchen, without resorting to exotics to make something special. Of course we can use exotics too, but let's not overlook the huge scope of what we can do with basics.
- My own taste (for the last time, hurrah!) is to eat healthy food most of the time, without unnecessary fats, and to make it delicious using healthy additives. And I eat some unhealthy stuff too, for a bit of variety and for my immune system. Now it's your turn: but do remember that we can make healthy every bit as delicious as unhealthy.

No Waste
- Really a subset of Taste: everything we throw away is lost taste, whether it's lost washing up that extra pan or by boiling the taste out and then throwing it down the drain.
- Using extra pans to cook ingredients separately creates waste, and makes each of our meat, veg and potatoes into a dish on its own. Instead of having one balanced dish with multiple flavours, we will be judged on different dishes, each served on the same plate, but without help from the others' flavours. We make extra work for ourselves and increase the chances of someone finding fault: family fun for masochists.

Haste
- Dare to undercook: it's so easy to leave things in for too long, so that they lose their texture and start to burn. Do we need to waste precious minutes creating disaster out of triumph? I'm sure we've better things to do.

No Paste
- Do the decent thing by your ingredients and let their native texture shine through; get rid of that food processor, if you ever had one.

I've listed four concepts to capture different aspects, but really they all come down to Taste in the end. No surprise here: we are talking about Food.

Cooking is creative: much of the satisfaction comes from creating a delicious meal out of different component parts: the whole is greater than the sum of its parts. This satisfaction can be in the physical dexterity of making something particularly tricky and doing it well: for example the ultimate soufflé or spun-sugar cage. Or it can be in the making of something new, starting with the ingredients we have to hand and adding others as we build the dish to our taste: the process is absolutely organic and instantaneous. Or it could be both: *Jette Cuisine* in a spun-sugar cage.

I've always found making up new meals to be much more satisfying – as well as less time-consuming – than regurgitating other peoples' ideas. But it's extraordinary how many otherwise capable people insist "Oh I couldn't possibly do that: I haven't got any imagination" or other self-deprecating excuse. As we can now see, it's not so much about having imagination as using the ingredients we have to hand and mixing them to arrive at a taste and effect we want on the day. As we said in Chapter 1, we all know whether we prefer sugar in coffee or ketchup with our burger, one lump or two, so we can all add ingredients to achieve a taste. This book just gives a bit of guidance as to how we can extend the concept of adding ketchup or mustard into adding any ingredient in the kitchen. Then we just watch as the meal makes itself.

It's amazing how a few minutes of creative cooking after a hard day at the office can regenerate us. Everyone has days when nothing goes right, and we all need to feel worthwhile. We all need to eat every day too, and a quick blast of *Jette Cuisine* serves both purposes, with minimal washing up afterwards. It's good for the soul, every day, ultimately it will cheer anyone up.

Whatever chefs may try to tell us, good food doesn't have to be complicated; we only need to be a little bit smart to realise this and put it into effect on a daily basis. Otherwise it's too much like hard work. *Jette Cuisine* is bigger than that, and exemplifies a philosophy of turning what we have to our advantage, rather than being distracted by what we haven't. Self-reliance and belief are simple when we learn to question people who think they know better. Challenging stuff, but beyond this book, so enough!

Would I leave you without a Recipe? Would I ever! Rules are not there to be broken, but they all have their exceptions, and this is mine. This was given to me by my University Director of Studies at his summer drinks party, and with hindsight it's probably influenced my cooking out of all proportion to the ingredients it uses. I don't know what it was called, (as a recipe it must have a name) so let's call it:

Some Are Number

Ingredients: Dry White Wine (the driest we can get)
                 Clear Fizzy Lemonade
                 Cucumber

Method:
       Half-fill a jug with chilled white wine, and add a few thin slices of cucumber. Top up with an equal quantity of chilled lemonade, stir gently and serve.

We can of course add all sorts of other ingredients like mint leaves, fruit, brandy, absinthe, that bright stuff we brought back from holiday, but this misses the point: as the alcohol content is low, it can be poured down in summer without too many ill effects. The most important ingredient is the cucumber, which makes the drink taste as if it's been spiked. So everyone feels and acts as though they're getting much merrier than they are, and no one gets a sore head.

The ultimate *Jette* drink: quick, simple and effective.

Good Health!

APPENDIX
Lost Mine When I Was Three

Disaster! The Wife thinks I should put in a couple of recipes, just to get things started. She thinks the culture shock will be too great.

And the views of Senior Management should never be ignored. Completely, anyway.

So if you Dear Reader, like her, are reeling from information overload, this little Appendix is for you, to guide you through the first steps to discovery that cooking really is that easy. And some of the culture shocks we may need to bridge are:

• Zhetted Vegetables	That Tasty
• Undrowned Pasta	So Simple
• Underdone Steak	So Succulent
• Cheese & Jam	Individually
• Bread Tricks	Totally Textural
• Oats	Oatstanding

I'll go through each of these step-wise, referring you back to the main text for any extra background so that I'm not duplicating what's gone before.

I'm still not going to give you any recipes, and this is not because I'm just being bloody-minded. It's because I don't know your circumstances, how many you're cooking for, what food you have in. But it's mainly because I DON'T KNOW HOW.

I don't know how many hunfies (or handfuls if you prefer) of pasta will feed a family of five. It depends on how hungry they are and what else we add. And as we don't eat pasta with our hands, I can't even translate that into quantities. So how are we to gauge how much?

After a lot of thought, I've come to the conclusion that I base my quantities on the size of the pan I cook in. Cheap saucepans (as we get from the supermarket) come in Small, Medium & Large. (They're also called things like 6" & 8", but I've got two 8" pans at home that are quite different in size/shape, so I suggest we stick with Small, Medium & Large; you know which I mean.)

Base your quantities on how much you fill your saucepan, and how big it is. Here's how:

Feeding	Small Pan	Medium Pan	Large Pan
One	Half-Full	Quarter-Full	Cover Bottom
Two	Full *	Half-Full	Third-Full
Three	-	Nearly Full	Half-Full
Four	-	Full *	Three-Quarters
Five	-	-	Full
Six	-	-	Full *

Table of Saucepans

These quantities are based on a mixture of carbohydrate, vegetables and protein in the same pan; a complete meal in one. And "Full" doesn't mean spilling out over the stove: leave a bit of height for stirring or boiling. "Full * " with an asterisk means that these portions are adequate rather than generous, at least by my family's standards.

I can't emphasise how important it is that you do your thing, and discover that your way is better than anything someone else can tell you. Why should it not be? No reason why not. Don't be fazed: things will turn out different from what you expect; that's what learning's all about (if it was expected, you'd know it already.)

So my suggestion is to try these things out first in small quantities, on your own or with your partner. Don't wait till you've got a hungry family of six or a dinner party for twelve and then say "I think I'll just give that *Jette Cuisine* a blast". Or if you do, you're a more reckless gambler than I am.

When you're not in a rush (so you can take time to see what's happening), try these out.

Dutch Pasta for Two *(see also Pasta Section p40)*
You'll need:
- Some Pasta (anything compact like quills, twists or macaroni, ie not spaghetti or lasagne)
- Dutch smoked sausage
- An onion
- A few mushrooms
- Milk or tinned tomatoes (your choice)
- Some hard cheese (like Cheddar, not processed like Edam)
- Water

What's also nice is:
- A few herbs
- A few green beans
- Red wine
- Grainy mustard
- Salt & pepper

Pasta is such an easy friendly meal, it seems a shame to try it out on your own. (But of course you can, halve the quantities. Or double for a family of four.) Read this bit through before starting.

Take a Medium saucepan. Look at our Table of Saucepans above: it wants to end up about half-full for two people. Of which about half wants to be pasta, which will double in size during cooking, so you mathematicians will have worked out the pan wants to be one-eighth full of dry pasta to start with. Hey: just chuck some in so that you can't see the bottom of the pan. Cover with boiling water from the kettle (that means just to the top of the dry pasta when it's shaken level, no higher), bring back to the boil, a quick stir to make sure the pasta doesn't stick, lid on and turn the heat down.

Chop an onion, and put it in with the pasta, lid back on. With dried herbs if you want. (Check how the pasta's growing, it probably hasn't by much at this stage, but you get an idea how many more ingredients you need to add to get your pan up to half-full.) Take a smoked pork sausage (the one they call "Dutch"), chop half of it into the pan and save the rest. Or chop in the whole lot, I don't mind.

How full is the pan? The pasta should be expanding now, make sure it doesn't boil dry, but don't add water: some mushrooms will help, and you can chop in a few green beans as well if you like. How about a splash of red wine from the wine box? Always add flavour. Keep it moist rather than drowned: you don't want to throw out any liquid, or boil off excess; enough liquid to be succulent rather than soup.

I'm giving you two choices for the sauce: red or white. The red is a tin of tomatoes, the white is milk.

> Red: Squeeze in the juice from the tin, chop the tomatoes (if they're whole) and put them in.
> White: Pour in a little milk to keep the mixture moist, and a bit of grainy mustard: about a teaspoonful?

By now, the pasta should be about done, your pan should be half-full (or more!). Chop some cheddar cheese slices, just a couple for red sauce to add texture, twice as much for the white (cheese) sauce. Stir this in (lid off!) until it's melted and then turn the heat off. (Don't boil the cheese, it'll go stringy.) Spoon into bowls and serve, with salt & pepper.

What have you learned?
- How pasta expands and thickens its own sauce.
- How you throw nothing away.
- How other ingredient flavours blend into the mix, but each still tastes in its own right.
- How mushrooms add moisture.

- How tomato juice gets absorbed by the pasta.
- How a splash of red wine adds flavour without dominating.
- How milk gets thickened by the pasta.
- How cheese thickens and glazes a sauce as well as flavouring it.
- How easily cheese stirs in as soon as it's melted, so it doesn't need boiling (spoiling).

Quite a lot really. Why not have a bit of salad with it?

Side Salad for Two *(see also Salads Section p87)*
You'll need:
- Lettuce, tomatoes, cucumber, peppers, any combination of these or any salad vegetables you like. (You can get ready-chopped out of a packet of you prefer.) Enough for two small bowls (or side-of-plates).
- A little red wine, either out of a box or a bottle you're drinking.
- Grainy mustard.
- Salt & pepper.
- A slice of toast.

What's also nice is:
- A few fresh herbs
- Jam!

The main point here is the dressing: put a tablespoonful of red wine in a cup and mix in half a teaspoonful of grainy mustard. Quick taste, then add salt and/or pepper bit by bit to taste; the salt's more important here. If your wine makes this too bitter, stir in a tiny bit of jam (use the tip or handle of the teaspoon to scoop a little from the jar) to taste.

When you've chopped your salad into a bowl, pour your red wine dressing over the top and stir it in. If there's not enough dressing for your quantity of salad, make up a bit more, the same quantities but this time do it straight into the salad, now you know you can play with the taste. Don't mind the colour, it makes the salad look like it's got exotic leaves in it. (Or you can use white wine instead.)

Put half the salad into a separate bowl, leaving any excess dressing behind in the first bowl. Notice how the salad you've transferred has taken only a little dressing with it, perhaps not enough.

Now back to the first bowl (the one with the extra dressing.) Toast a slice of bread, white or brown, it doesn't matter, chop it into cubes and stir half of it into the first bowl of salad. Notice how the toast absorbs the dressing and lifts it into the salad. If you need more toast, stir in the other half of the toast cubes; if not, feed them to the birds.

Result? You've got two salads: one to accompany your pasta, and another more substantial that will do as a light meal on its own. I don't pretend that dressing is the best you've ever have eaten, or can do in future, and I've certainly tasted worse in restaurants or bottled. But red wine, salt, mustard and jam? Who'd've thought it. Just don't go driving afterwards!

What have you learned?
- How you can make salad dressings without relying on oil and vinegar.
- How wine combines sharp acidity with smoothness and body.
- How adding salt and spice converts wine into a fully-fledged ingredient.
- How a little jam corrects sourness without having to taste like a butty.
- How toast absorbs excess dressing and lifts it into the salad.
- How to make a salad into a light meal.
- The confidence to make the dressing with the salad: you don't need that cup!

Perhaps you think I'm overstating the lessons learned, but each of them is there, to be stored and used in future.

And some time in the future, you'll want another meal, so try:

Meat & Veg   *(see also Vegetables & Proteins Sections p14 & p64)*
You'll need:
- A carrot (size doesn't matter)
- An onion (size doesn't matter)
- A few mushrooms
- A slice of cheap steak
- Oil

What's also nice is:
- Cabbage (a leaf)
- Celery (a stick)
- Green beans
- Peppers
- Garlic
- A few herbs
- Salad tomatoes
- Splash of red wine
- Salt & pepper
- A sprinkle of oatmeal
- A little cheese

200gm (or 8oz) of steak with the above is enough for two, and will cook in a medium (or large) saucepan. Put about a teaspoonful of oil in the (non-stick) pan. If your steak has fat on it, trim it off and either throw it away or chop it into little bits and fry it in the oil in your pan: it'll make more grease for you!

Wipe your carrot clean, trim the ends off and chop it up finely, the peel as well. Put it in the pan, turn on the heat underneath, put the lid on and shake the pan to get the oil over the carrot pieces. Turn the heat down when you hear it start to sizzle (that's the steam, remember).

Peel the onion, chop it finely and put it in the pan with the carrot; stir; lid back on. (A sliced cabbage leaf subs out the onion and gives texture; a chopped celery stick adds a slight peppery taste; both good added with the onion but not essential. If you've got beans, cut them into manageable bits and add to the pan after a couple of minutes.) Slice your mushrooms, but don't add them yet.

Slice your steak into strips about 2cm x 1cm x ½cm (small thin strips to you and me). Now add your mushrooms to the pan, stir and replace lid. Any peppers can go in now too. And garlic, and herbs. After about a minute, add your steak strips and stir about for about 10sec to make sure all the meat has seen the bottom of the pan and is distributed through the vegetables. Lid back on for about a minute, then stir it again: if you can't see any red bits of meat, it's ready to serve. You can leave it a bit longer if you want, but DON'T OVERDO IT! Stir in a chopped salad tomato if you like, and/or a splash of red wine, taste a little, add salt/pepper to taste, then put on plates. You can stir in a couple of slices of cheese, chopped, or add it as a garnish after serving and let it gently melt as you eat it; or not.

What have you learned?
- How to zhet vegetables, how they make their own moisture, and how good they taste.
- That you don't have to peel carrots!
- How mushrooms (and peppers and tomatoes) add liquid.
- How even the cheapest steak can be tender and succulent if you don't try too hard.
- How vegetables keep steak moist and stop it burning.
- How meat adds to the flavour of the vegetables.
- How all the ingredients are still recognisable in a single dish.
- How the whole is greater than the sum of its component parts.

You can try the same vegetables without the steak, just to prove that they don't need the meat, they still taste good on their own. Try sprinkling on a bit of oatmeal just before serving: see how it absorbs excess liquid and adds a bit of crunch to the texture. Try adding blue cheese instead of cheddar. There are more variations here than I can write down: you choose.

If you're still hungry after that lot, try:
Oats & Honey   *(see also Oats Sections p107)*
You'll need:
- Oat flakes, or oatmeal, or both
- Runny honey

I'm assuming you're going to have a mug of tea or coffee after this, so why not do it in the same mug, then the drink will wash away any leftovers? Fill the mug about a quarter full of dry oats (part flakes and part oatmeal if you have both) and mix a teaspoonful of clear honey in with them. At first you think one teaspoonful is never going to be enough honey, but as you stir you find that it is; try more oats next time, see how far the honey goes! When the mixture is all one consistency, it's ready to eat.

What have you learned?
- How a little honey goes a long way.
- How oats stop the honey making the inside of the mug sticky.
- How simple and healthy can also be delicious.

Enjoy your coffee afterwards; any little bits of oat left over are a bonus!

Simple isn't it? Now that you've worked through these examples, you've covered all the strange culture shocks I mentioned at the start of this Appendix. Try out at least one idea from each main chapter as well (see below); better still, bend it to suit yourself. Remember: it's your (and your guests') taste that counts, no one's else.

You'll be delighted at how clever you are, although I won't be in the least surprised.